Leading from Day One

I0050484

Leading from Day One

The Essential Guide for New Supervisors

Jeff Ogren

BEP

BUSINESS EXPERT PRESS

Leader in applied, concise business books

Leading from Day One:
The Essential Guide for New Supervisors

Copyright © Business Expert Press, LLC, 2026.

Cover design by Onur Burc

Interior design by S4Carlisle Publishing Services, Chennai, India

All rights reserved. No part of this publication may be reproduced, stored in a retrieval system, or transmitted in any form or by any means—electronic, mechanical, photocopy, recording, or any other except for brief quotations, not to exceed 400 words, without the prior permission of the publisher.

First published in 2025 by
Business Expert Press, LLC
222 East 46th Street, New York, NY 10017
www.businessexpertpress.com

ISBN-13: 978-1-63742-870-2 (paperback)
ISBN-13: 978-1-63742-871-9 (e-book)

Human Resource Management and Organizational Behavior Collection

First edition: 2025
10 9 8 7 6 5 4 3 2 1

EU SAFETY REPRESENTATIVE
Mare Nostrum Group B.V.
Mauritskade 21D
1091 GC Amsterdam
The Netherlands
gpsr@mare-nostrum.co.uk

Dedication

For the original Sunshine Group—Leila, Elyse, and Kira. And for our faithful rescue companions—Missy, and in loving memory of Akko and Inca.

You have joined me across continents and oceans, embracing each new adventure with grace and wonder. Through every move, every challenge, and every triumph, your unwavering support has been my anchor. Together we've discovered that home isn't a place—it's wherever we are together.

We've sacrificed much but gained infinitely more. Your love and patience have made this journey—and this book—possible.

Like everything else in my life, this work is better because of you.

With all my love and gratitude.

Description

Leading from Day One: The Essential Guide for New Supervisors **provides a comprehensive roadmap for professionals transitioning into their first leadership role.**

Drawing from over 25 years of international human resource experience, this practical guide addresses the most common challenges new supervisors face: shifting from individual contributor to team leader, building trust, setting clear expectations, managing time effectively, and handling difficult conversations.

Each chapter combines research-backed principles with real-world examples, providing actionable strategies for immediate implementation. Readers will learn how to create psychological safety, delegate effectively, lead through change, and build a culture of continuous improvement. Unlike theoretical leadership books, this playbook offers step-by-step guidance with worksheets and reflection exercises that transform concepts into practice.

Whether you're preparing for your first supervisory role or looking to strengthen your leadership foundation, this essential resource will help you navigate the critical transition from colleague to confident, respected leader.

Acknowledgments

I am deeply grateful for the guidance and mentorship of four extraordinary leaders who have profoundly shaped my journey as a supervisor and professional.

Jill Perry, an exceptional human resources professional, has revolutionized HR training and led the oversight of locally employed staff policy for the U.S. Department of State. Her expertise and innovative approaches have set new standards in the field. Judy Marcoullier has been a cherished friend, mentor, and teammate since our graduate school days. From swapping notes in grad school to collaborating on HR training initiatives across continents, our friendship and professional partnership has enriched both my life and career. Lenton Davies, a consummate professional and trusted confidant, has been an invaluable sounding board through numerous challenges, particularly when navigating difficult leadership situations. His wisdom and integrity exemplify what it means to be both a gentleman and a scholar. Don Kilburg, PhD, brother, friend, author, and leader in AI, has provided influence and guidance that has been instrumental in many of life's adventures. His insights have opened new perspectives on leadership in our rapidly evolving professional landscape.

All four have provided instrumental feedback in completing this book, offering constructive guidance that has strengthened its content and message. More importantly, they have helped shape the leader and supervisor I am today. Their mentorship, friendship, and unwavering support remain among my most treasured professional gifts.

I am also grateful to the countless colleagues, team members, and organizations across multiple countries who have taught me that leadership transcends borders, cultures, and languages. Every challenge we faced together became a lesson; every success we shared became a building block.

Finally, thank you to every early-career professional who will read this book. Your willingness to lead from day one—regardless of your title or tenure—is what will shape the future of our workplaces and our world.

Contents

Introduction: Welcome to Leadership!

Leading a team is a lot like juggling—if you drop a ball, it's not just embarrassing; it could be a disaster! And by "juggling," I mean trying to keep your cool while everyone throws unexpected questions and complex challenges your way, making you wonder if you should have pursued that dream of becoming a professional scuba diver instead.

The transition from individual contributor to supervisor is one of the most significant career shifts you will face. It's not merely an increase in responsibility; it requires a fundamental change in how you approach your role within the organization. Previously, your success was measured by your own achievements—the tasks you completed and the projects you delivered. Now, as a supervisor, your success is determined by the performance and growth of your team. This shift demands the development of new skills: leadership, communication, delegation, prioritization, strategic thinking, and emotional intelligence.

With over 20 years of experience managing and leading diverse teams, I have witnessed firsthand the unique challenges and rewarding moments that come with stepping into a supervisory role. The path is often fraught with uncertainty as new supervisors grapple with letting go of their former solo roles and embracing their leadership responsibilities. The weight of expectations can be overwhelming, especially when faced with the nuances of team dynamics and the imperative to foster a positive work environment.

A Funny Misstep

Let me share a little story from my early days of supervision—one that still makes me chuckle (and cringe) to this day. Fresh into my new supervisory role, I was eager to make a mark. After all, I had spent years excelling at my tasks and felt I knew the ropes inside and out.

One day, our team was tasked with completing a major project under a tight deadline. I wanted to ensure everything was perfect, so I decided to jump in and take charge. I ended up redoing a colleague's work on a key presentation because I felt it needed a "supervisor's touch." As I feverishly made edits, I imagined the accolades I'd receive for ensuring our team looked top-notch.

However, the moment I presented the finished product, I was met with blank stares. It turned out I had changed the central message without consulting anyone, completely derailing the intent of the project! My team had worked hard on their sections, and here I was, a "supervisor," doing the very thing I was supposed to empower them to handle. The look on their faces was a mix of shock and disbelief. Afterward, one brave team member asked, "So, when do we get to show you **our** work?"

This experience taught me an invaluable lesson: As a supervisor, it's no longer about focusing on output—my own output—but rather on the team's outcome. The essence of my role was to support my team, allowing them to take ownership while I provided guidance. Patience became my new mantra as I learned to let go of the need for control and trust my team to deliver their best work.

The Essence of Leadership

Leading a team effectively means cultivating an environment where individuals feel valued and motivated. I have learned that the essence of leadership lies not in exerting authority but in empowering others. As a seasoned management professional, I have facilitated countless transitions for individuals taking their first steps into supervisory positions. Each journey has reinforced a critical truth: The most successful supervisors understand that their role is to enable others to thrive.

This book will explore the common challenges faced by first-time supervisors, such as letting go of day-to-day tasks, shifting from peer to leader, and balancing short-term needs with long-term goals. These challenges are often accompanied by feelings of self-doubt and anxiety as new supervisors navigate their dual responsibility of driving team performance while simultaneously building their leadership capabilities.

Before diving into the specific skills and strategies of supervision, it's essential to understand the fundamental concepts that form the foundation of effective supervision. Let's introduce a few key terms, basic principles, and core concepts that will appear throughout the book, so we can fully engage with the material.

What Is Supervision?

At its core, supervision is the art and science of guiding others to achieve organizational goals. A supervisor serves as the vital link between management and frontline employees, translating organizational objectives into actionable tasks while supporting team members' growth and development.

Key Terms and Concepts

Management versus leadership: Management focuses on organizing, planning, and controlling resources to achieve specific objectives. Leadership involves inspiring, guiding, and developing people to reach their full potential. Effective supervisors must balance both roles.

Organizational hierarchy: Understanding where supervisors fit within the organizational structure and how information and authority flow through different levels of management.

Span of control: The number of employees directly reporting to a supervisor. This can vary based on industry, complexity of work, and organizational structure.

The Evolution of Supervision

The role of a supervisor has evolved significantly over the past century:

Traditional Model (1900s–1950s)
> The traditional model of supervision emerged during the Industrial Revolution and was heavily influenced by Frederick Taylor's Scientific Management principles (Taylor 1911). Supervisors

functioned primarily as taskmasters, focusing on strict oversight and control of workers to maximize efficiency. This era was characterized by clearly defined hierarchies, rigid work schedules, and standardized procedures. Supervisors measured success through output metrics and compliance with established protocols, with little consideration for worker well-being or input. The relationship between supervisors and workers was largely authoritarian, with communication flowing strictly top–down. This approach proved effective for the mass production needs of early industrialization but often led to worker dissatisfaction and high turnover.

Human Relations Model (1950s–1980s)

Following the famous Hawthorne Studies and the work of Elton Mayo (Mayo 1949), supervision underwent a significant transformation with the Human Relations Model. This approach recognized that workers were not merely economic beings but social creatures with complex needs and motivations. Supervisors began incorporating psychological and social factors into their management style, paying attention to group dynamics, employee satisfaction, and workplace relationships. The model emphasized two-way communication, employee feedback, and the importance of informal workplace groups. Supervisors were trained to consider morale, job satisfaction, and personal growth as key factors in productivity. This period saw the introduction of employee counseling, team-building activities, and more participative management styles.

Modern Approach (1980s–Present)

The modern approach to supervision represents a synthesis of previous models while adapting to contemporary workplace challenges. This model recognizes that effective supervision requires situational flexibility and a balanced focus on both productivity and people. Supervisors are expected to be coaches and facilitators rather than just overseers, helping employees develop their potential while achieving organizational goals. The approach emphasizes emotional intelligence, cultural awareness, and adaptive leadership styles. Modern supervisors must navigate complex challenges, including remote work, diverse teams, rapid technological change, and shifting workforce expectations. They are expected to foster innovation, manage knowledge workers, and create inclusive environments while maintaining operational excellence. This model also incorporates concepts like servant leadership, transformational leadership, and authentic leadership, reflecting a more sophisticated understanding of how to motivate and lead in contemporary organizations.

Contemporary research has significantly expanded upon the foundational work of early management scholars like Drucker (1954) and Follett (1949), revealing that effective supervision in today's workplace requires a more comprehensive skill set. Studies from leading institutions, including Harvard Business School and the Society for Human Resource Management (2022), demonstrate that successful supervisors must master an integrated framework of competencies. These include traditional technical expertise and interpersonal skills, while also encompassing digital literacy, cultural competence, change management capabilities, and the ability to create psychologically safe work environments. This expanded understanding reflects the increasing complexity of the modern workplace and the evolving demands placed on supervisory roles.

Core Competencies for Modern Supervisors

Successful supervisors consistently demonstrate proficiency in several key areas that form the foundation of effective leadership. While the specific demands of the role may vary across industries and organizational settings, five core competencies remain essential to supervisory success:

1. Technical competence: Supervisors must understand the work they oversee, including key processes, tools, and industry-specific knowledge. This foundational expertise enables credible leadership, informed decision-making, and effective support for team members. While supervisors don't need to be the foremost technical experts, they must grasp the essentials to guide their teams with confidence.

2. Interpersonal skills: The ability to build strong relationships and communicate clearly is critical to fostering trust, resolving conflicts,

and motivating team members. Effective supervisors listen actively, adapt their communication to various audiences, and create an environment where collaboration and psychological safety can flourish.

3. Planning and organization: Supervisors are responsible for aligning team efforts with organizational goals. This involves managing resources efficiently, setting priorities, coordinating tasks, and establishing systems that enable timely, high-quality results. Strong planning and organizational skills ensure that teams operate with clarity, structure, and focus.

4. Problem solving: Whether navigating day-to-day challenges or addressing more complex issues, supervisors must think critically, assess situations accurately, and make sound decisions. Effective problem solving includes identifying root causes, evaluating options, and implementing practical, sustainable solutions.

5. Leadership: Beyond technical and managerial capabilities, supervisors must also inspire confidence, provide direction, and support the growth of their team members. Effective supervisors lead by example and foster an environment where others can thrive.

Together, these competencies enable supervisors to manage people, performance, and priorities with confidence and clarity. They serve as the bedrock of effective supervision and are essential for navigating the evolving demands of today's workplace.

The Supervisor's Role in Modern Organizations

Today's supervisors face unique challenges that their predecessors didn't encounter, making the transition into supervision particularly demanding for first-time leaders. These challenges require new supervisors to develop sophisticated management approaches while learning to navigate complex organizational dynamics

Remote and Hybrid Work Environments
New supervisors must master virtual leadership skills and develop strategies for maintaining team cohesion across physical distances. This includes learning to build trust without regular face-to-face

interaction, ensuring equitable treatment between remote and office-based staff, and creating effective virtual communication protocols. First-time supervisors often struggle with maintaining team visibility and measuring productivity in these distributed environments.

Multigenerational Workforces

Modern workplaces typically span four or five generations, each with distinct work styles, communication preferences, and career expectations. New supervisors must learn to bridge these generational gaps while avoiding stereotypes and leveraging the unique strengths of each generation. This requires developing flexible management approaches and fostering cross-generational collaboration.

Rapid Technological Change

Supervisors must not only stay current with evolving technology but also lead their teams through digital transformation initiatives. First-time supervisors often face the dual challenge of managing their own learning curve while supporting team members who may resist technological change or require extensive training and support.

Increased Focus on Diversity, Equity, and Inclusion

Despite recent political winds, modern supervisors are expected to create inclusive environments that support diverse teams. This requires developing cultural competence, recognizing and addressing unconscious bias, and ensuring fair treatment in all aspects of team management. New supervisors must learn to navigate sensitive conversations and advocate for equity while building team unity.

Greater Emphasis on Work-Life Balance

Today's supervisors must balance organizational productivity goals with increasing demands for flexibility and work-life integration. This includes managing flexible schedules, setting appropriate boundaries, and supporting employee well-being while maintaining team performance. First-time supervisors often struggle to find this balance for themselves while helping their teams do the same.

Studies by Gallup (2022) indicate that the supervisor's role has become increasingly complex, with 70 percent of team engagement variance tied to the quality of supervision. This statistic underscores the critical importance of providing new supervisors with comprehensive training and support as they navigate these modern challenges. Success in today's supervisory roles requires continuous learning, adaptability, and a commitment to developing both technical and interpersonal leadership skills.

For first-time supervisors, these challenges are particularly acute as they must simultaneously develop their leadership identity while mastering these complex responsibilities.

Common Myths About Supervision

Before proceeding, let's address some common misconceptions:

Myth 1: Good individual contributors automatically make good supervisors.
Reality: Different skills are required for supervision than for individual contribution.
Myth 2: Supervisors must know how to do everything their team does.
Reality: While technical knowledge is valuable, the ability to lead and develop others is more important.
Myth 3: Supervision is about controlling people.
Reality: Modern supervision focuses on empowerment and guidance rather than control.

The Transition Journey

The shift from individual contributor to supervisor represents one of the most significant career transitions, requiring fundamental changes in perspective, skills, and behaviors:

Mindset Shift: From Doing the Work to Enabling Others
New supervisors must transition from being the "doer" to becoming the "enabler." This involves learning to delegate effectively, trust team members' abilities, and resist the urge to micromanage or simply do the work themselves when challenges arise. Many

first-time supervisors struggle with letting go of their expert status and accepting that their success now comes through others' achievements.

Time Management: From Personal to Team Productivity

The supervisor role demands a dramatic shift in how time is allocated and prioritized. Instead of focusing on individual tasks and deadlines, supervisors must learn to balance team oversight, mentoring, strategic planning, and administrative responsibilities. This often means sacrificing the immediate satisfaction of completing personal tasks for the longer-term rewards of developing team capabilities.

Communication: From Peer-to-Peer to Leader-Team Dynamics

New supervisors must develop more sophisticated communication skills, learning to articulate vision, provide clear direction, give constructive feedback, and manage difficult conversations. They must also navigate the delicate balance of maintaining professional boundaries with former peers while building strong leader-team relationships. This includes mastering both one-on-one and group communication in various formats, from casual check-ins to formal performance reviews.

Accountability: From Self to Team Results

Perhaps the most challenging transition is accepting responsibility for the entire team's performance. New supervisors must learn to define success through collective achievements rather than personal accomplishments. This includes developing systems for monitoring team progress, addressing performance issues, and creating an environment that promotes both individual and team success.

Identity Development: From Technical Expert to People Leader

An often-overlooked aspect of the transition is the psychological journey of developing a leadership identity. New supervisors must reshape their self-perception and learn to derive satisfaction from different types of achievements than those that earned them the promotion.

Research from the Center for Creative Leadership (2023) reveals significant challenges for new supervisors. Their studies found that 20 percent of first-time managers are performing poorly according to their subordinates, while 26 percent of these managers admit they weren't ready to lead others when promoted. Even more concerning, almost 60 percent report never receiving any training when transitioning into their first leadership role. These statistics underscore why so many new supervisors experience significant stress and uncertainty during their first 18 months, particularly regarding the interpersonal and emotional aspects of leadership. However, there is hope: organizations that provide structured transition support through mentoring, leadership development programs, and clear role expectations see new supervisor success rates improve by up to 40 percent.

Using This Book Effectively

To get the most from this playbook:

1. Read sequentially: Chapters build upon each other, providing a structured learning journey.
2. Complete the worksheets: Practical exercises help solidify learning and build confidence.
3. Reflect and apply: Take time to consider how concepts apply to your specific situation.
4. Review and revisit: Use the book as a reference guide throughout your supervision journey.

A Journey of Growth

While the transition to a supervisory role may be daunting, it also represents one of the most rewarding changes in a career. Witnessing the growth and development of your team can provide a profound sense of fulfillment. As you embrace your new role, approach it with a mindset of continuous learning. Leadership is not a destination but a journey—a journey that requires resilience, adaptability, and a willingness to evolve.

Embrace the shift, for it is in this transformative process that you will discover not just the leader within but also the potential for extraordinary team achievements. The tools and lessons within these pages are crafted not just to guide you but to inspire you to be the leader your team needs.

CHAPTER 1

Transitioning to a Supervisory Role

It's not the size of the team that matters, it's how you guide them. And by "guide," I mean… try not to panic when they ask you questions you don't have answers to.

The transition from individual contributor to supervisor represents one of the most significant and challenging career shifts professionals face. Research suggests that as many as 60 percent of new managers struggle or fail within the first two years of their role—often due to a lack of preparation, insufficient training, and inadequate support during the transition into leadership (Arruda 2023). This high failure rate stems from the fundamental transformation required—it's not merely about increased responsibility, but rather a complete reimagining of one's role within the organization.

As an individual contributor, success is measured through personal achievements, completed tasks, and delivered projects. However, the supervisor's success depends entirely on the performance and growth of their team. McKinsey & Company (2021) identified three core competencies critical for this transition: people management (38 percent of success factors), strategic thinking (32 percent), and emotional intelligence (30 percent). This data underscores the complexity of the role shift and the new skills required.

Time allocation also changes dramatically for new supervisors. While research shows most managers currently dedicate only about 7 percent of their time to people development, leadership experts recommend that effective supervisors allocate substantially more time to team development and strategic planning (Quantum Workplace 2022). This redistribution of time and energy often proves challenging for new supervisors who built their careers on technical expertise and individual achievement.

Perhaps most critically, Ibarra et al. (2018) demonstrate that successful transitions require a fundamental identity shift from "doer" to "enabler." While this transformation can feel overwhelming, it also presents one of the most rewarding career opportunities. Success requires understanding common challenges, embracing a leadership mindset, and developing a strategic approach to management.

Key Challenges of Transitioning and Skills for Success

Transitioning into a supervisory role is a significant career milestone, often accompanied by both excitement and apprehension. To navigate this transition successfully, new supervisors must overcome key challenges while cultivating essential leadership skills.

Letting Go of Day-to-Day Tasks

The Challenge

One of the most difficult adjustments for first-time supervisors is learning to let go of the daily tasks they previously managed. Many supervisors are promoted because they excelled as individual contributors, which can make it tempting to continue focusing on those familiar tasks. However, this limits a supervisor's effectiveness. Leadership is not about doing—it's about enabling others to perform and empowering your team to take ownership of their work.

Understanding the Shift

The mindset shift from "doer" to "leader" is critical. Your value as a supervisor is no longer defined by your individual output but by how effectively you guide your team toward shared goals. Research in organizational psychology has shown that supervisors who delegate and focus on strategic oversight foster higher levels of team engagement and performance.

Essential Skill: Delegation and Empowerment

Delegation is more than assigning tasks; it's about empowering team members to take ownership of their responsibilities. Effective delegation requires knowing your team's strengths and weaknesses, setting clear expectations, and providing the necessary follow-up to ensure tasks are completed.

Example

Sarah, a development team lead at TechCorp, initially struggled to transition from coder to leader. By focusing on mentoring her team and establishing clear processes, she empowered her team members to excel in their roles, allowing her to focus on strategic priorities.

Challenges and Benefits

- Challenges: Letting go of tasks can feel uncomfortable, and many new supervisors fear losing control or trust in their team.
- Benefits: Empowered employees are more engaged, and effective delegation frees supervisors to focus on long-term goals.

Shifting from Peer to Leader

The Challenge

Supervising former peers is often one of the most complex transitions for a new leader. Managing relationships with individuals who were once equals requires establishing authority while maintaining trust and respect.

Essential Skill: Emotional Intelligence (EI)

EI, once considered a "soft" skill, is now widely recognized as a critical driver of leadership success. Popularized by Daniel Goleman (1995), EI is the ability to recognize, understand, and manage your own emotions while effectively influencing the emotions of others. For supervisors, particularly those transitioning into leadership roles, EI is indispensable. Research underscores its impact:

Performance: A study by TalentSmart found that emotional intelligence accounts for 58 percent of performance in all types of jobs, highlighting its significant role in workplace success (TalentSmart 2023).

Retention: Companies that prioritize emotional intelligence have observed a 20-percent increase in productivity and employee satisfaction (Vorecol 2024).

Conflict Reduction: Organizations implementing EI training reported a 30-percent reduction in workplace conflicts within six months, demonstrating the effectiveness of EI in fostering a harmonious work environment (PsicoSmart 2024).

Why EI Matters for First-Time Supervisors

The transition to supervision requires navigating complex interpersonal dynamics, managing authority shifts, and building trust in a new role. EI equips supervisors to:

Build Trust Through Self-Awareness

- Recognize and manage your own emotional reactions to challenges.
- Understand how your new authority influences team dynamics.
- Maintain composure during difficult conversations.
- Model the emotional maturity you expect from your team.

Navigate Team Dynamics

- Read subtle social cues and anticipate potential conflicts.
- Adapt communication styles to individual team members.
- Create psychological safety to encourage open dialogue.
- Foster a collaborative environment where concerns can be addressed constructively.

Lead Through Transition

- Acknowledge and address team concerns about leadership changes.

- Balance assertiveness with empathy when setting expectations.
- Maintain professional boundaries while preserving relationships.
- Handle resistance and challenging feedback with grace and clarity.

Practical Implementation: The First 90 Days

To integrate EI into your leadership approach, adopt a structured strategy for the critical first 3 months of your supervisory role:

Weeks 1 to 30: Building the Foundation

- Conduct individual meetings to understand each team member's:
  - Work style and preferences.
  - Career aspirations.
  - Concerns about the transition.
  - Communication preferences.
- Actively listen and take notes to demonstrate your commitment to understanding and supporting your team.

Weeks 31 to 60: Establishing Communication and Feedback

- Implement regular feedback channels, such as weekly one-on-one meetings.
- Establish team communication protocols to ensure transparency and alignment.
- Define decision-making processes to clarify roles and responsibilities.

Weeks 61 to 90: Solidifying Dynamics and Strategy

- Review and adjust your leadership approach based on team feedback.
- Strengthen team relationships and dynamics through trust-building initiatives.
- Begin implementing strategic changes aligned with both team and organizational goals.
- Develop long-term growth plans for team members, demonstrating your investment in their success.

Key Takeaway: EI Is Actionable and Transformative

EI is not about avoiding difficult decisions—it's about handling them more effectively. Supervisors with high EI balance empathy with accountability, creating environments where individuals thrive, conflicts are minimized, and trust is built.

Developing EI requires deliberate practice, just like any other leadership skill. By focusing on self-awareness, communication, and empathy, you can foster stronger relationships, improve team performance, and navigate challenges with confidence.

Remember: Your success as a supervisor depends not just on what you do, but how you do it. The investment you make in understanding and managing emotions—both yours and your team's—will pay dividends in building a cohesive, high-performing team.

Balancing Short-Term Needs with Long-Term Goals

The Challenge

First-time supervisors are often caught between immediate operational demands and broader strategic planning. Balancing these priorities is essential for sustaining both short-term success and long-term growth.

Essential Skill: Prioritization and Time Management

Supervisors must develop time management skills and focus on aligning daily tasks with long-term objectives. Delegating operational responsibilities enables supervisors to dedicate time to strategic planning.

Example

A manufacturing supervisor balanced daily production oversight with implementing a new efficiency system by delegating routine tasks to their team. This approach ensured both immediate productivity and future improvements.

Challenges and Benefits

- Challenges: Balancing priorities can lead to burnout if not managed carefully.

- Benefits: Effective delegation and time management create a sustainable work environment and empower teams to contribute to long-term success.

Building and Applying Core Skills for Success

While addressing these challenges, first-time supervisors must also develop foundational leadership skills that enable them to succeed in their new role:

Emotional Intelligence

- Overview: EI helps supervisors build trust, resolve conflicts, and foster a positive work environment.
- Application: Use empathy and active listening to navigate interpersonal challenges.
- Example: A retail supervisor noticed a team member underperforming and, through a compassionate conversation, addressed the root cause and improved performance.

Self-Awareness

- Overview: Self-awareness helps supervisors understand their leadership style and adapt to their team's needs.
- Application: Reflect on your strengths and weaknesses to tailor your approach.
- Example: A nonprofit supervisor adapted her collaborative style to incorporate more structure for meeting deadlines.

Communication Skills

- Overview: Clear, transparent communication aligns teams and fosters collaboration.
- Application: Host regular team meetings to clarify expectations, address challenges, and ensure alignment.
- Example: A software development supervisor held daily stand-up meetings to keep the team focused and engaged.

Conclusion: Embrace the Shift

The transition from individual contributor to supervisor is both a challenging and rewarding journey. It requires a significant shift in mindset—from focusing on your own accomplishments to empowering the success of your team. This new role brings opportunities to inspire others, drive collective achievement, and contribute to your organization's long-term goals.

To navigate this transition successfully, focus on mastering the challenges of letting go of day-to-day tasks, shifting from peer to leader, and balancing short-term needs with long-term planning. At the same time, invest in developing the foundational skills that will support your leadership journey: EI, self-awareness, delegation, and communication. These tools will not only enhance your ability to lead effectively but will also build trust, cohesion, and motivation within your team.

Remember, leadership is not a destination but a continuous process of growth and learning. Every challenge is an opportunity to refine your approach and expand your capabilities. Embrace the shift, lean into the lessons that come with it, and maintain a mindset of curiosity and resilience.

Before moving on to the next chapter, take time to complete the accompanying worksheets. These exercises are designed to help you reflect on the concepts introduced here, assess your current strengths, and identify areas for growth. With each step, you'll build the confidence and skills needed to excel in your new role. Let the journey begin!

CHAPTER 2

Building Trust and Rapport with Your Team

Trust is fragile, like a sheet of paper—once it's crumpled, smoothing it out is never the same. So, handle it with care from the start.

As a first-time supervisor, your ability to build trust will determine your effectiveness more than any other factor. Trust is the cornerstone of effective leadership and the foundation for a high-performing team. Research, including Google's *Project Aristotle*, reveals that **psychological safety**—the confidence team members have to take risks, voice concerns, and share ideas without fear—is the critical differentiator between high- and low-performing teams. Without trust, even the most talented teams falter.

Let's explore how new supervisors can establish trust, avoid common pitfalls, and create an environment where psychological safety enables success.

Four Critical Areas for Building Trust

1. **Demonstrate Reliability Through Consistent Actions**
   Trust begins with dependability. When your actions consistently align with your words, your team learns they can count on you.
   - Follow through on commitments, no matter how small.
   - Maintain regular one-on-ones without canceling.
   - Document decisions and agreements to ensure clarity.
   - Communicate changes early and transparently.
2. **Practice Transparent Leadership**
   Transparency fosters openness and reduces uncertainty within your team.
   - *Daily actions:*
     - Share the "why" behind decisions to provide context.

- Admit when you don't know something; humility builds credibility.
- Keep your team informed about organizational changes.
- Be clear about expectations, deadlines, and goals.

3. **Show Professional Vulnerability**

Vulnerability strengthens relationships by humanizing you as a leader.

- *How to do this effectively:*
    - Share challenges you face as you transition into your role.
    - Seek feedback on your leadership style and adjust based on input.
    - Acknowledge your team members' expertise and contributions.
    - Publicly learn from mistakes to model growth and resilience.

4. **Create Psychological Safety**

Psychological safety allows team members to feel secure in expressing themselves without fear of judgment or retaliation.

- *Practical steps:*
    - Respond positively to questions, concerns, and suggestions.
    - Protect team members who raise issues or take risks.
    - Publicly give credit for successes and address problems privately.
    - Encourage reasonable risk-taking and learning from failures.

The First 90 Days: A Roadmap for Building Trust

Though we just discussed a first 90-day roadmap, it cannot be stressed enough how critical these initial months are in your new supervisory role. I like to follow what I call the "90-Day Rule"—though I may not always need the full 90 days. I use this time deliberately to get to know my people, understand the problems, and familiarize myself with the policies of my new section before making any major decisions. During this period, my primary focus is on building trust, as trust is the foundation of effective leadership. Without trust, you have no currency. Without currency, you lack the ability to move the business of the section forward.

Expanding on the 90-day roadmap outlined earlier, this framework offers a structured approach to help you establish a strong foundation for collaboration, reliability, and psychological safety. By taking intentional steps and prioritizing trust-building during this critical phase, you can create an environment where your team feels supported, valued, and ready to thrive under your leadership.

Weeks 1 to 30: Establishing Your Foundation

- Schedule individual meetings to learn about each team member's work style, career goals, and immediate concerns.
- Document and address team needs to demonstrate responsiveness.
- Establish consistent communication patterns through regular check-ins and updates, building reliability.

Weeks 31 to 60: Developing Team Dynamics

- Begin regular team meetings with clear agendas to enhance transparency.
- Implement decision-making processes that incorporate team input.
- Delegate tasks with structured support to empower team members and build trust.
- Create collaboration opportunities to strengthen team cohesion.

Weeks 61 to 90: Strengthening Trust Through Action

- Review and deliver on early commitments to reinforce credibility.
- Act on feedback to show adaptability and responsiveness.
- Develop individual growth plans collaboratively, demonstrating investment in your team's success.

By adhering to this roadmap, you'll build the trust and relationships necessary to establish yourself as an effective leader while laying the groundwork for long-term team success.

Building Trust: A First-Time Supervisor's Guide to Success

Trust forms the bedrock of high-performing teams, and research confirms its profound impact. Harvard Business Review's (2022) study revealed that teams with strong trust foundations are 50 percent more productive and experience 74 percent less stress. For new supervisors, understanding how to build and maintain trust is perhaps your most critical leadership challenge.

Understanding Trust in Action

Trust manifests in observable behaviors across your team. When trust is present, you'll notice a natural flow of communication, with team members raising concerns early and openly sharing different viewpoints in meetings. This openness extends beyond formal settings—you'll see spontaneous collaboration, with team members helping each other without being asked and freely sharing knowledge across functions.

Performance metrics also reflect trust levels. Teams with high trust meet deadlines without constant oversight, solve problems at appropriate levels, and regularly generate innovative ideas. Most tellingly, you'll notice fewer escalations to upper management as team members feel empowered to handle challenges within their scope.

Active Listening: The Foundation of Trust

Active listening is more than simply hearing words—it's a deliberate practice of full engagement with both the speaker and their message. For new supervisors, mastering this skill creates the psychological safety needed for open communication and trust. Let's break down the HEAR method with practical examples:

Hold space: This means giving your complete attention to the speaker without interruption or distraction. In practice, this looks like:

- Closing your laptop during one-on-ones
- Turning your phone face down
- Maintaining appropriate eye contact
- Using affirmative body language (nodding, facing the speaker)

For example, when Sarah, a team member, comes to discuss a project challenge, resist the urge to check e-mails or glance at your phone. Instead, turn your chair to face her fully, maintain natural eye contact, and demonstrate through your body language that she has your complete attention.

Engage with questions: Ask thoughtful questions that deepen understanding rather than directing the conversation. Effective questions might include:

- "Could you tell me more about how that impacted the project?"
- "What do you see as the main obstacle here?"
- "How do you think we might approach this differently?"

Imagine a team member expresses frustration about a recurring issue. Instead of jumping to solutions, you might ask, "What aspects of this situation are most challenging for you?" This encourages deeper exploration and shows you value their perspective.

Acknowledge emotions: Recognize and validate the emotions being expressed, whether positive or negative. This doesn't mean you have to agree, but rather that you understand. For instance:

- "I can see why that situation would be frustrating."
- "It sounds like you're really excited about this opportunity."
- "That must have been challenging to deal with."

When a team member shares anxiety about an upcoming deadline, acknowledge their feelings: "I understand why you're concerned about this timeline. It is ambitious, and your commitment to quality shows in your concern."

Reflect key points: Summarize what you've heard to ensure understanding and show engagement. Use phrases like:

- "Let me make sure I understand correctly…"
- "What I'm hearing is…"
- "So from your perspective…"

For example: "So from what you've shared, there are three main concerns: the timeline feels too tight, you need additional resources for testing, and you're worried about team burnout. Have I captured that correctly?"

Putting It All Together: A Real-World Example

Here's how a complete active listening interaction might look:

Team member: "I'm worried about the new project management software rollout. The team is already stretched thin, and I don't think we have the bandwidth to learn a new system right now."

Supervisor response:

1. Hold space: *Turns away from computer, faces team member, and maintains eye contact*
2. Engage: "What specific aspects of the rollout concern you the most?"
   Team member: "Well, we're in the middle of three major projects, and learning new software takes time we don't have. Plus, some team members are still struggling with our current system."
3. Acknowledge: "I hear your concern about the timing, and it makes sense that you're thinking about the team's current workload and capabilities."
4. Reflect: "Let me make sure I understand—you're concerned about introducing new software when the team is already managing multiple projects, and you're particularly worried about the learning curve given some existing challenges with our current system. Is that accurate?"

The impact: When you consistently practice active listening, you'll notice:

- Team members come to you more frequently with ideas and concerns.
- Problems are surfaced earlier when they're easier to address.
- Innovation increases as people feel heard and valued.
- Team engagement improves as trust builds.

Building Trust Through Active Listening and Empowerment

Active listening serves as your foundation for trust-building, transforming routine interactions into opportunities for deeper connection. The

HEAR method (Hold space, Engage with questions, Acknowledge emotions, and Reflect key points) offers a practical framework that demonstrates respect for your team's expertise while gathering crucial insights. By implementing this method consistently, you create an environment where team members feel genuinely heard and valued.

This investment in listening naturally evolves into empowerment. When team members experience being truly heard, they gain confidence to take on greater responsibilities. Begin this empowerment journey by delegating clearly defined projects with specific outcomes rather than prescribed methods. Establish strategic check-in points that provide support without micromanagement, allowing your team to develop their own approaches and solutions. Create an environment where reasonable mistakes aren't just accepted but are recognized as valuable learning opportunities.

The key is to provide resources and support proactively, demonstrating your commitment to your team's success before they have to ask. This approach creates a positive cycle of trust: As your team experiences your confidence in their abilities, they develop greater trust in their own capabilities and judgment. Similarly, as you witness their growth and success, your trust in their decision-making strengthens.

Remember that building trust through active listening and empowerment is an ongoing journey, not a destination. Start with small steps in both areas, celebrate progress, and remain consistent in your approach. The long-term rewards—stronger relationships, increased innovation, and improved team performance—make this investment in trust-building one of your most valuable activities as a supervisor.

Avoiding Trust-Breaking Behaviors

Trust forms the bedrock of high-performing teams, and unethical behavior quickly erodes that trust. According to Gallup's *State of the Global Workplace* research, nearly one in four U.S. employees reported firsthand knowledge of unethical behavior in their workplace within the past year. Employees who witnessed such behavior were 2.7 times more likely to be actively disengaged and 2.3 times more likely to report experiencing burnout (Kemp 2024). For new supervisors, this highlights a vital lesson: trust isn't just built through positive actions, but preserved by avoiding damaging behaviors and upholding ethical standards in every decision and interaction. Remember that trust builds gradually through consistent, thoughtful actions rather than grand gestures. According to McKinsey & Company (2023a), trust—particularly psychological safety—is a foundational element in high-performing organizations. Teams that feel safe to speak up, share ideas, and take risks without fear of retribution are more likely to collaborate effectively, innovate consistently, and remain resilient through change. As a new supervisor, investing in trust-building behaviors—such as transparency, accountability, and active listening—will yield long-term dividends in team performance, creativity, and engagement.

Case Study: Building Trust Through the Peer-to-Leader Transition

When Sarah was promoted from senior developer to team lead, she faced a challenge familiar to many new supervisors: transitioning from peer to leader while building trust with her eight-person development team.

Initial Challenges

- Team members hesitated to share problems, fearing judgment.
- Former peers struggled with the authority shift.
- Technical decisions were bottlenecked, requiring her input on even minor issues.
- Some team members subtly resisted her leadership.

Trust-Building Approach

Sarah implemented a three-part strategy:

1. Active listening: She began with individual "listening sessions," applying the HEAR method:
   - Holding space for each team member to speak freely

- Engaging with thoughtful questions about their work and concerns
- Acknowledging their feelings about the transition
- Reflecting back their perspectives to ensure understanding

2. Clear decision frameworks: She created a "decision rights" matrix that:
   - Specified which decisions team members could make independently
   - Outlined when to consult peers versus escalate to her
   - Provided clear parameters for technical choices
   - Established backup plans for risk management

3. Gradual empowerment: She built team confidence through:
   - Starting with smaller technical decisions
   - Increasing decision-making scope as confidence grew
   - Celebrating independent solutions, even when different from her approach
   - Using mistakes as learning opportunities rather than failures

Results

After 6 months, the team showed marked improvement:

- Technical decisions were made confidently without unnecessary escalation.
- Communication became more open and proactive.
- Innovation increased as team members felt safer taking risks.
- Project delivery accelerated due to reduced bottlenecks.

Key takeaway: Trust-building requires consistent action over time. Through active listening, clear frameworks, and gradual empowerment, Sarah transformed team dynamics from hesitation and dependence to confidence and collaboration.

For new supervisors, this case demonstrates that successful leadership transitions don't happen overnight. Focus first on understanding your team through active listening, then build trust through clear expectations and steady empowerment.

Conclusion: Building Trust—Your Foundation for Success

Trust is not just another leadership skill—it is the foundation upon which all effective supervision is built. Leadership practitioners emphasize that trust is cultivated through consistent, thoughtful behaviors rather than one-time gestures. For example, Devin Vodicka (2020) highlights four elements that contribute to effective trust-building: consistency in behavior, competence in one's role, open communication, and genuine care for team members' well-being. As a new supervisor, your ability to master these elements will define both your immediate success and long-term effectiveness as a leader.

Throughout this chapter, we've explored how trust transforms groups into high-performing teams. McKinsey's (2023b) research reinforces this, emphasizing that trust-based leadership fosters environments where team members feel safe to innovate, take calculated risks, and solve problems collaboratively. While specific metrics may vary, the real power of trust lies in its ability to create an environment where team members feel safe to innovate, take calculated risks, and solve problems collaboratively.

We've seen that building trust requires a deliberate approach focused on:

- Mastering active listening through the HEAR method, demonstrating genuine care
- Creating clear frameworks that showcase your competence and empower decision making
- Maintaining consistent behavior and communication patterns
- Demonstrating appropriate vulnerability while maintaining professional boundaries
- Measuring trust through team behaviors and performance indicators

The case study of Sarah's transition from peer to leader illustrates a crucial truth: Trust-building is not about grand gestures but rather consistent, thoughtful actions that demonstrate reliability, transparency, and respect. Her success came from intentionally incorporating all four trust elements—showing competence in her technical leadership, maintaining consistent behavior patterns, establishing open communication channels, and demonstrating genuine care for her team's growth and well-being.

Remember that trust is fragile—it takes time to build and can be quickly damaged. Every interaction, decision, and communication either strengthens or weakens the trust your team places in you.

By approaching your new role with patience, authenticity, and a commitment to building genuine connections, you create an environment where both your team and your leadership can thrive. Focus on maintaining consistency in your actions, continuously developing your competence, fostering open communication, and showing genuine care for your team members' success and well-being.

Looking ahead to the next chapter, we'll explore how to effectively communicate your vision and set clear expectations, building on this foundation of trust to create a truly high-performing team environment. Before we begin, be sure to review the worksheets associated with this chapter.

CHAPTER 3

Setting Clear Expectations and Providing Feedback

Managing a team without clear expectations is like playing charades in the dark—nobody knows what's happening, and everyone ends up frustrated.

If you do not provide your team with clear expectations, you undermine both performance and engagement. Research shows that organizations with well-defined performance standards consistently outperform their peers in productivity, employee satisfaction, and retention (McKinsey & Company 2024).

As a new supervisor, establishing clear expectations and providing effective feedback are foundational leadership skills. When expectations are unclear, even the most talented individuals may struggle to deliver results. Similarly, without regular, constructive feedback, team members lack the guidance needed to grow and improve. This chapter explores practical strategies for setting clear expectations and delivering effective feedback that drives performance and engagement.

Establishing Clear Performance Expectations

According to Gallup (2023), only 45 percent of employees strongly agree they know what's expected of them at work. This lack of clarity undermines productivity, lowers engagement, and leads to missed opportunities for growth. While specific outcomes vary by organization, the research emphasizes that clear expectations are essential for aligning performance, motivating teams, and improving the overall employee experience.

The Foundation of Effective Supervision

The Three Levels of Expectations

Setting clear expectations is fundamental to effective supervision. Expectations provide structure, guide performance, and ensure alignment between individual contributions and organizational goals. To create a well-functioning team, supervisors must establish three key levels of expectations: foundational expectations, performance goals, and growth expectations. Each of these plays a distinct role in defining what is required, measuring success, and fostering long-term professional development.

Foundational Expectations: Defining the Core Responsibilities

Foundational expectations establish the baseline for success by defining core job responsibilities, professional conduct, and quality standards. These expectations clarify what is required of employees in their day-to-day roles and helping them understand their primary duties and the behaviors necessary for a productive work environment. Communication protocols and team norms also fall under this category, ensuring that employees interact effectively and collaborate efficiently. For example, in a customer service role, foundational expectations might include response time requirements, communication standards for engaging with clients, and escalation procedures for handling complex issues. When employees clearly understand these expectations, they are more likely to perform consistently and contribute to a stable, efficient workplace.

Performance Goals: Driving Results Through Measurable Targets

Performance goals translate organizational objectives into specific, measurable targets that drive accountability and productivity. These expectations go beyond job descriptions and establish clear performance indicators that enable employees to assess their progress. By linking individual contributions to team and company success, supervisors ensure that employees understand how their work impacts the broader organization. Metrics such as increasing quarterly revenue by 15 percent through targeted outreach initiatives or reducing project turnaround times by 20 percent help employees focus their efforts and measure achievements. Performance goals create a sense of ownership and accountability, allowing supervisors to track progress and provide meaningful feedback based on objective criteria rather than subjective observations.

Growth Expectations: Fostering Development
and Long-Term Success

While foundational expectations and performance goals address immediate responsibilities and measurable outcomes, growth expectations focus on long-term professional development. These expectations encourage employees to expand their skill sets, explore leadership opportunities, and engage in continuous learning. Supervisors play a crucial role in supporting professional development by establishing structured initiatives such as cross-training programs, mentorship opportunities, and leadership development courses. For instance, an employee in a technical role may be encouraged to learn new programming languages to enhance team capabilities. Growth expectations not only benefit individual employees by increasing their career potential but also strengthen the organization by ensuring a skilled and adaptable workforce.

By establishing and maintaining these three levels of expectations, supervisors create an environment where employees know what is required, understand how their work contributes to the organization, and have opportunities for professional advancement. Clarity in expectations leads to higher engagement, improved performance, and a stronger commitment to achieving both personal and organizational success.

The SMART Goal Framework

Setting effective goals requires a structured approach. The SMART framework provides a clear methodology to ensure that goals are well-defined, achievable, and aligned with organizational objectives. SMART stands for Specific, Measurable, Achievable, Relevant, and Time-bound—each component playing a crucial role in crafting objectives that drive individual and team success.

(S) Specific: Defining Clear Objectives

The first step in setting a SMART goal is ensuring specificity. A specific goal clearly defines what needs to be accomplished, leaving no room for ambiguity. It answers fundamental questions such as Who is responsible? What needs to be achieved? Where will this take place? When should it happen? Why is it important?

For example, rather than stating a broad objective like "Improve customer service," a more specific goal would be: "Reduce customer response time to under four hours by implementing new tracking software." This refined goal provides clear direction and establishes a measurable target, making it easier for employees to focus their efforts effectively.

Clarity in goal setting helps employees understand expectations, reduces misinterpretations, and ensures that all team members are working toward the same outcome. When objectives are well-defined, employees feel more confident in their ability to meet expectations, leading to better overall performance.

(M) Measurable: Tracking Progress and Defining Success

Measurable goals include concrete criteria for evaluating progress. Without measurable benchmarks, it becomes difficult to assess whether a goal has been achieved or to track progress along the way. Establishing specific key performance indicators (KPIs) allows supervisors and employees to monitor outcomes and make necessary adjustments.

For example, instead of setting a vague goal such as "Increase customer satisfaction," a measurable goal would be: "Increase customer satisfaction ratings from 85% to 90% within 6 months." This goal incorporates a quantifiable metric, allowing managers to track improvements and provide targeted feedback.

Measurability is crucial for motivation and accountability. Employees can track their progress, celebrate milestones, and stay engaged in their objectives. Additionally, supervisors can provide meaningful support and recognition when specific milestones are reached, reinforcing a result-oriented work culture.

(A) Achievable: Setting Realistic and Challenging Goals

While ambitious goals can drive performance, they must also be realistic. Achievable goals strike the right balance between ambition and feasibility, ensuring that employees are challenged but not set up for failure. When setting a goal, it is essential to consider available resources, time constraints, and external factors that may impact success.

For instance, a sales team may have historically achieved a 10 percent increase in revenue annually. Aiming for a 15 percent increase in 6 months through expanded marketing efforts may be ambitious but remains within the realm of possibility. However, setting a goal of doubling revenue in the same timeframe may be unrealistic and demotivating.

Achievable goals promote confidence and engagement. Employees are more likely to stay motivated when they believe success is within their reach, and supervisors can provide the necessary support to help them overcome challenges along the way.

(R) Relevant: Aligning Goals with Organizational Objectives

A relevant goal is one that aligns with broader organizational priorities and contributes to the team's overall success. Goals should be meaningful and directly connected to the strategic direction of the company. When employees understand the relevance of their goals, they feel a greater sense of purpose and commitment to their work.

For example, if a company aims to reduce customer churn, an individual goal might be: "Reduce customer churn by 20 percent through enhanced onboarding procedures." This goal directly supports the company's long-term retention strategy, ensuring that individual contributions are meaningful and aligned with larger business objectives.

Relevance also fosters engagement by helping employees see the impact of their work. When goals are clearly connected to the company's success, employees are more likely to take ownership and remain invested in achieving them.

(T) Time-Bound: Creating Urgency and Accountability

Every goal must have a deadline to create a sense of urgency and maintain momentum. Time-bound goals provide a clear timeframe for completion, ensuring that progress is continuously monitored and adjustments are made as needed. Without deadlines, goals risk becoming open-ended aspirations rather than actionable objectives.

A well-defined time-bound goal might be: "Launch new product features by the end of Q2." This statement establishes a clear deadline, allowing teams to plan their workload accordingly and track progress at key milestones.

Time constraints also prevent procrastination and help prioritize tasks. Supervisors can implement regular check-ins to assess progress, address challenges, and ensure that the team stays on track. When employees have a clear timeline, they can manage their workload more effectively and maintain productivity.

Final Thoughts on SMART Goals

The SMART framework provides a structured approach to goal setting, ensuring clarity, accountability, and alignment with organizational priorities. By defining Specific, Measurable, Achievable, Relevant, and Time-bound goals, supervisors can create a work environment that fosters motivation, efficiency, and success.

When applied effectively, SMART goals empower employees to take ownership of their tasks, track progress with confidence, and contribute meaningfully to the organization's objectives. Supervisors who embrace this framework can enhance team performance, drive strategic initiatives, and build a culture of continuous improvement.

The Three Pillars of Effective Leadership

Leadership experts like Patrick Lencioni emphasize the importance of organizational clarity and consistent communication as foundational to successful team management. In his work, Lencioni argues that when leaders provide clear expectations, reinforce key messages, and align team behaviors around shared goals, teams are more likely to remain motivated, productive, and cohesive. I have combined these insights into three essential elements for successful expectation-setting and team management: clarity, context, and consistency. Each of these pillars plays a critical role in ensuring that teams are aligned, motivated, and productive (Lencioni 2022).

Clarity: Setting Clear and Measurable Expectations

Clarity is the foundation of effective leadership. Employees perform best when they have a precise understanding of their responsibilities, expected outcomes, and performance benchmarks. Clear expectations remove ambiguity, reduce misunderstandings, and enhance accountability.

Supervisors should define success criteria explicitly and use concrete examples to illustrate performance standards. For instance, instead of simply instructing a team to "improve response times," a clear directive would be: "Respond to customer inquiries within 24 hours with a 90 percent satisfaction rating." Providing measurable benchmarks helps employees stay focused and motivated while making performance evaluations more objective and transparent.

Context: Connecting Individual Contributions to the Bigger Picture

Employees are more engaged when they understand how their work contributes to the organization's overall mission. Context helps employees see the purpose behind their tasks and reinforces their role in achieving team and company goals.

Supervisors should consistently communicate the "why" behind expectations. For example, linking faster customer response times to increased retention rates and revenue growth highlights the tangible impact of high performance. Sharing relevant business insights and strategic priorities ensures that employees feel connected to the broader organizational vision and are motivated to contribute meaningfully.

Consistency: Maintaining Steady Performance Standards

Consistency in leadership fosters stability and trust within a team. When performance expectations shift frequently or are enforced inconsistently, employees may become frustrated or disengaged. Establishing regular check-ins, maintaining steady performance standards, and updating priorities transparently create a structured and predictable work environment.

Supervisors should implement structured feedback mechanisms, such as weekly team meetings, to review goals and address challenges. Consistent communication reinforces expectations, provides opportunities for course correction, and ensures alignment between individual efforts and organizational objectives.

By integrating clarity, context, and consistency into leadership practices, supervisors create a high-functioning team environment where employees understand their roles, recognize the impact of their contributions, and feel supported in their professional growth. However, setting expectations alone is not enough—supervisors must also provide effective feedback to reinforce these expectations and guide performance.

Delivering Effective Feedback

Feedback is crucial for guiding performance and ensuring expectations are met. Gallup's research indicates that employees who receive meaningful feedback in the past week are significantly more engaged—80 percent report being fully engaged. Additionally, employees who receive daily feedback from their managers are 3.6 times more likely to strongly agree they are motivated to do outstanding work (Gallup 2021). This underscores the importance of timely and meaningful feedback in enhancing employee motivation and team performance.

The Situation–Behavior–Impact (SBI) Model

Providing effective feedback is an essential skill for supervisors, and the situation–behavior–impact (SBI) model offers a structured approach to delivering it. This model helps ensure that feedback is clear, objective, and actionable by breaking it down into three key components: situation, behavior, and impact.

Situation: Setting the Context

The first step in delivering feedback is to describe the specific situation in which the observed behavior occurred. By providing context, the supervisor helps the employee understand exactly when and where the behavior took place. This eliminates ambiguity and ensures that feedback is relevant and timely.

For example, rather than saying, "You didn't contribute much in the meeting," a more structured approach would be: "During yesterday's client presentation, when the team was discussing project milestones…" Clearly defining the situation makes it easier for the employee to recall and reflect on the event.

Behavior: Identifying Observable Actions

Once the situation is established, the next step is to describe the employee's specific actions. This should be based on observable behaviors rather than interpretations or assumptions. Constructive feedback focuses on what was done rather than making subjective judgments.

For instance, instead of saying, "You weren't engaged in the discussion," a supervisor using the SBI model might say: "You remained silent when the client asked for input on the next steps." This approach keeps feedback fact-based and actionable.

Impact: Explaining the Consequences

The final step in the SBI model is to explain how the behavior impacted the team, the client, or the organization. Employees need to understand the broader effects of their actions so they can make necessary adjustments.

For example, rather than saying, "That was unhelpful," a more effective statement would be: "Because you didn't provide input, the client expressed concerns about whether we had a clear plan moving forward." This explanation connects actions to their outcomes, encouraging employees to reflect on their behavior and its implications.

By consistently applying the SBI model, supervisors can foster a culture of clear communication, continuous improvement, and professional growth. This structured approach ensures that feedback remains constructive, encouraging employees to develop their skills while reinforcing positive contributions.

Common Pitfalls to Avoid

When providing feedback and setting expectations, supervisors should be mindful of common pitfalls that can undermine effectiveness. Avoiding these issues ensures that feedback is constructive, actionable, and well-received.

The Feedback Sandwich: Avoiding Diluted Messages

A well-intentioned but flawed approach to feedback is the "feedback sandwich," where constructive criticism is placed between two positive statements. While this method may seem like a way to soften criticism, it often leads to confusion. Employees may focus only on the positive aspects and overlook the necessary areas for improvement. Additionally, it can make positive reinforcement feel insincere when it is consistently paired with criticism.

Instead of sandwiching constructive feedback between praise, supervisors should be direct and solution-focused. Separating recognition from improvement discussions ensures that both types of feedback maintain their intended impact. Constructive feedback should be framed around specific observations and paired with actionable steps for improvement. For example, rather than saying, "You did great on the project, but you need to work on meeting deadlines. Still, you contributed great ideas," a better approach would be: "Your contributions to the project were insightful and helped move it forward. However, missing the deadline impacted our delivery schedule. Let's discuss strategies to improve time management moving forward."

Vague or Subjective Feedback: Providing Clear and Actionable Guidance

Another common mistake in feedback is being too vague or subjective. Statements like "You need to improve" or "Your work isn't quite there yet" lack clarity and do not provide employees with the information needed to make meaningful changes. Employees benefit from specific, actionable recommendations that outline exactly what needs improvement and how they can achieve it.

For instance, instead of saying, "Your presentations need work," a more effective approach would be: "Your presentations could be more engaging by incorporating more data-driven visuals and summarizing key points concisely. Let's schedule a session to go over effective presentation techniques." Providing concrete examples and measurable criteria for success helps employees understand expectations and make tangible improvements. Feedback should always include guidance on how to improve and an opportunity for employees to ask questions and seek clarification.

Cultural Insensitivity: Adapting Feedback for a Diverse Workforce

Providing feedback in a culturally diverse work environment requires sensitivity and adaptability. Different cultures have varying norms around giving and receiving feedback. For example, some cultures expect direct, straightforward feedback, while others may prefer a more indirect and diplomatic approach. A failure to consider these differences can lead to misinterpretation and discomfort.

Supervisors should take the time to understand cultural nuances and adapt their feedback style accordingly. This includes being aware of language barriers, nonverbal communication differences, and the preferred methods of critique in different cultures. For instance, in some cultures, public criticism may be perceived as particularly harsh, whereas in others, it may be more accepted. A best practice is to discuss feedback in private settings when addressing areas for improvement and to ensure that feedback is delivered with respect and clarity. Emphasizing shared goals and offering support helps build trust and encourages open communication in multicultural teams.

By recognizing and avoiding these common pitfalls, supervisors can ensure that their feedback is well-received and drives positive change. Effective feedback is direct, specific, and culturally aware, helping employees develop professionally while maintaining morale and engagement.

Managing Difficult Feedback Conversations

Providing constructive feedback can be challenging, particularly when addressing performance issues or areas for improvement. A structured approach ensures that difficult feedback conversations remain professional, effective, and solution-focused. Managing these discussions involves three key stages: preparation, delivery, and follow-up.

Preparation: Laying the Groundwork for Effective Feedback

Before initiating a difficult feedback conversation, preparation is essential. Supervisors should gather specific examples of the behavior or performance issue in question to ensure the discussion is fact-based rather than subjective. Vague feedback can lead to confusion or defensiveness, while concrete examples provide clarity. Additionally, preparing key talking points helps keep the conversation focused and productive.

Choosing the right timing and setting is equally critical. Feedback should be given in a private, professional environment where the employee feels comfortable discussing the issue openly. Delivering difficult feedback in a rushed or inappropriate setting can lead to misunderstanding and resistance. Thoughtful preparation ensures that feedback conversations are constructive rather than confrontational.

Delivery: Communicating with Clarity and Professionalism

During the feedback conversation, it is crucial to remain focused on facts and maintain a professional tone. Emotionally charged or accusatory language can put employees on the defensive, reducing their receptiveness to the message. Instead, feedback should be framed around observable behaviors and their impact on the team or organization.

Active listening is also essential during this stage. Giving employees an opportunity to share their perspective fosters a two-way dialogue and can provide valuable context that may not have been previously considered. Encouraging employees to express their thoughts and concerns ensures that they feel heard, which in turn increases the likelihood that they will engage constructively with the feedback.

Follow-Up: Reinforcing Accountability and Growth

After delivering feedback, it is important to document key points discussed during the conversation. Keeping a record ensures clarity and accountability while also serving as a reference for future performance evaluations. Following up with an improvement plan that includes clear action steps helps employees understand the path forward.

Regular check-ins should be scheduled to monitor progress and provide ongoing support. These follow-ups allow supervisors to assess whether improvements are being made, address any new challenges, and reinforce positive changes. When handled effectively, difficult feedback conversations become opportunities for growth, strengthening both individual performance and overall team dynamics.

Case Study: From Goal Setting to Success— A New Supervisor's Journey

When Alex was promoted to marketing supervisor, the challenge seemed straightforward: increase website traffic by 30 percent over the next quarter. However, like many new supervisors, Alex quickly discovered that achieving organizational goals requires more than just delegating tasks— it demands a systematic approach to both goal setting and feedback.

The Initial Challenge

Alex inherited a team of five content creators, including several former peers. Beyond the traffic target, Alex faced common new supervisor challenges:

- Transitioning from peer to leader
- Translating broad objectives into actionable goals
- Building trust while maintaining accountability
- Creating effective feedback mechanisms

Setting the Foundation: SMART Goals in Action

Rather than simply announcing targets, Alex began with a team workshop. "Before we dive into numbers," Alex explained, "I want to understand how each of you sees our path to success." This collaborative approach yielded valuable insights about team capabilities and concerns.

The team then broke down the 30 percent traffic increase into specific components:

Specific: They identified three key content types that historically drove traffic:

- Blog posts (12 planned for the quarter)
- Social media campaigns (eight planned)
- Case studies (four planned)

Each content type had clear ownership and success metrics.

Measurable: Using analytics software, they established weekly tracking for:

- Content production rates
- Traffic growth
- Engagement metrics
- Search engine optimization (SEO) rankings

"Now," Alex explained, "we'll always know exactly where we stand."

Early Feedback Challenges

Alex's first attempt at addressing missed deadlines revealed the importance of structured feedback. When Sarah, a former peer, fell behind, Alex's initial approach proved problematic:

First Attempt: "Sarah, you know I hate bringing this up, but as your friend…"

After learning about the SBI model, Alex revised the approach:

Improved Version: "During the past two weeks (situation), I've noticed three blog posts were submitted after deadline (behavior). This has caused our design team to work overtime and delayed our publication schedule (impact). Can we discuss what's causing these delays and how I can help?"

The response difference was immediate. Sarah opened up about struggling with SEO requirements, leading to targeted training that improved both quality and timeliness.

Adapting and Growing

Midway through the quarter, data revealed an unexpected trend: social media posts were driving more traffic than blog posts. Alex used this insight to adjust the team's SMART goals:

- Reduced blog posts from 12 to 10
- Increased social campaigns from 8 to 10
- Implemented a shared project tracker

More importantly, Alex's feedback approach evolved to match team needs:

Morning quick-checks: Brief, informal conversations replaced rigid daily meetings, making feedback feel more natural.

Weekly metrics reviews: 30-minute data-driven discussions kept everyone aligned with goals while providing opportunities for immediate feedback.

Monthly development talks: One-on-one sessions focused on career growth and skill development, connecting individual aspirations to team objectives.

Success Through Structure

By quarter's end, the team had exceeded expectations:

- 35 percent increase in website traffic
- 40 percent reduction in missed deadlines
- 90 percent team satisfaction with feedback processes
- 25 percent improvement in content engagement

Team member perspectives revealed why the approach worked:

Sarah (content creator): "The specific goals made success measurable, while regular feedback helped me stay on track. When Alex discussed improvements, it felt focused on growth rather than criticism."

Michael (content creator): "Having clear metrics and consistent check-ins meant I always knew where I stood. The adjusted goals showed that our input mattered."

Key Lessons for New Supervisors

1. Start with structure—clear frameworks for goals and feedback provide consistency and reduce uncertainty.
2. Make it collaborative—involve your team in goal setting to ensure buy-in and realistic targets.
3. Use data wisely—regular metric reviews keep discussions objective and highlight needed adjustments.
4. Adapt your approach—be willing to modify both goals and feedback methods based on results and team needs.
5. Focus on growth—use feedback to build capabilities, not just correct issues.

Alex's experience demonstrates that successful supervision requires both clear direction and effective communication. By combining SMART goals with the SBI feedback model, new supervisors can create an environment where both individuals and teams thrive.

Conclusion: Building a Culture of Clear Expectations and Feedback

The journey from individual contributor to effective supervisor hinges on mastering two fundamental capabilities: setting clear expectations and providing meaningful feedback. Research consistently demonstrates the impact of these skills—while only 45 percent of employees clearly understand what's expected of them (Gallup 2023). Additionally, employees who receive frequent and meaningful feedback are significantly more engaged and motivated to perform at high levels—those receiving daily feedback are 3.6 times more likely to strongly agree they are motivated to do outstanding work (Gallup 2021).

Key Elements of Success

1. Clarity Drives Results
   - Set specific, measurable objectives
   - Provide concrete examples and guidance
   - Maintain transparent communication channels
2. Structure Enables Consistency
   - Utilize frameworks like SMART and SBI
   - Establish regular check-ins and reviews
   - Document expectations and feedback
3. Feedback Creates Growth
   - Foster two-way communication
   - Build trust through constructive dialogue
   - Encourage continuous improvement
4. Flexibility Sustains Progress
   - Adapt approaches based on team needs
   - Adjust goals as circumstances change
   - Remain open to new methods and ideas

The SMART framework and SBI model provide practical tools that transform these concepts from theory into action. When implemented thoughtfully, these approaches create a structured, supportive environment where employees feel empowered to perform at their best. Clear expectations reduce uncertainty, while well-delivered feedback encourages growth and improvement.

Remember that leadership is a journey of continuous learning. You won't get every interaction perfect, and that's acceptable. What matters is maintaining consistency in your approach while remaining flexible in your execution. By focusing on clear expectations and meaningful feedback, you create an environment where both your team and your leadership can thrive.

As a former mentor once said to me, "Clear expectations and consistent feedback aren't just management tools—they're the language of leadership." With these foundational skills in place, you're well-equipped to tackle more complex leadership challenges and drive sustained success for both your employees and your organization.

Looking ahead, these capabilities will serve as building blocks for developing and motivating your team members effectively. The journey from setting expectations to achieving results may not always be smooth, but with these tools and approaches, you have the framework needed to guide your team toward exceptional performance. Now, use those worksheets to build muscle memory!

CHAPTER 4

Managing Time and Priorities

Time management is all about balance—like juggling flaming swords while riding a unicycle. But the key isn't just to look cool doing it—it's making sure you don't get burned.

Managing time effectively is critical for supervisors, particularly those transitioning into their first leadership role. The shift from focusing solely on personal productivity to overseeing both one's work and the performance of others introduces a unique set of challenges. Supervisors must balance competing demands, navigate conflicting priorities, and ensure that their time is spent on high-value tasks that align with organizational goals.

The transition from individual contributor to effective supervisor involves redefining productivity and managing time effectively. While specific statistics vary, research indicates that new managers often grapple with increased workloads and feelings of decreased productivity during their initial year. This paradox highlights the core challenge of supervisory roles: Success is no longer measured by personal productivity alone, but by the collective achievement of your team.

The Shifting Landscape of Time Management

One of the most immediate and jarring transitions for new supervisors is how dramatically their relationship with time changes. As individual contributors, success is often tied to task completion, personal efficiency, and hands-on problem-solving. But in a supervisory role, time must be reallocated to managing others, aligning team efforts, and focusing on long-term goals. This shift requires not only a change in priorities but a fundamental rethinking of what it means to be productive.

Studies reveal that many supervisors struggle to adapt. Research from Proaction International (2021) suggests that managers, on average, spend 47 percent of their time in meetings and administrative tasks, 21 percent managing crises, 19 percent in active supervision, and only 13 percent on training and coaching their teams. Similarly, McKinsey's *State of Organizations 2023* report highlights that new supervisors frequently invert what would be considered an ideal distribution of time—spending up to 50 percent of their day on low-leverage, reactive tasks like paperwork and firefighting. This imbalance leaves little room for the strategic thinking and team development that actually define long-term supervisory success (McKinsey & Company 2023).

The Orchestra Conductor Effect

Think of stepping into a supervisory role as becoming the conductor of an orchestra. Previously, you might have been an accomplished violinist, focused solely on perfecting your part. Now, your success depends on coordinating multiple players, ensuring harmony across sections, and maintaining the overall tempo and direction of the performance.

This metaphor illustrates three critical shifts in time management:

1. From individual to collective focus—Your time must now serve the team's productivity rather than just your own. Research shows that supervisors who make this shift successfully see 35 percent higher team performance rates.
2. From tactical to strategic thinking—The scope of your time horizon must expand from daily tasks to longer-term planning and development. Studies indicate that supervisors who allocate at least 40 percent of their time to strategic activities lead teams that are twice as likely to exceed performance targets.
3. From doing to enabling—Success now comes through facilitating others' work rather than doing it yourself. Data shows that supervisors who master this transition achieve 45 percent better team engagement scores.

The Cost of Poor Time Management

The stakes are high. According to Gallup's research, ineffective time management by supervisors has measurable consequences on employee outcomes. Poor prioritization and unclear expectations can drive up stress, lower engagement, and reduce both productivity and innovation. Gallup's *State of the American Workplace* report found that managers account for 70 percent of the variance in team engagement, underscoring their central role in influencing workplace outcomes (Gallup 2017). More recently, Gallup's 2023 analysis on time management and productivity emphasized the direct relationship between how supervisors prioritize their time and how effectively teams perform (Gallup 2023). The ability—or inability—to manage time strategically is not just a personal challenge for supervisors; it's a determining factor in overall team success.

The goal isn't perfect time management—it's intentional time investment that drives both team success and personal growth. To achieve this, supervisors need a structured approach to prioritization that helps them focus on what truly matters.

The Eisenhower Matrix

Overview and Historical Context

One of the most effective tools for prioritization is the Eisenhower Matrix (Ng 2024), also known as the Urgent-Important Matrix. This powerful decision-making framework helps supervisors distinguish between tasks that demand immediate attention and those that contribute to long-term success. Named after Dwight D. Eisenhower, former U.S. President and Supreme Allied Commander during World War II, the matrix is rooted in his philosophy:

> *"What is important is seldom urgent, and what is urgent is seldom important."*

By using this framework, supervisors can shift from reactive task management to proactive leadership, ensuring that their time is spent on high-impact activities rather than constantly firefighting urgent but low-value tasks.

This principle remains a timeless strategy for leaders, especially supervisors who face a never-ending flow of requests, demands, and expectations. New supervisors often find themselves overwhelmed by "urgent" tasks, many of which have minimal strategic value. Competing demands often push leaders into a reactive "firefighting" mode, where they address immediate issues without considering their long-term impact. The Eisenhower Matrix provides a structured framework for decision making, enabling supervisors to focus on what truly matters while delegating, rescheduling, or eliminating less valuable activities.

Elements of the Eisenhower Matrix

Before exploring the four quadrants, it is crucial to understand the two core elements of the matrix: urgency and importance. These two factors dictate how tasks are categorized and ultimately determine the level of attention and action required for each task.

1. Urgency

Urgency refers to how quickly a task requires attention. Urgent tasks typically come with deadlines, time constraints, or immediate consequences for inaction. Urgency triggers a sense of pressure and compels action, often leading supervisors to "drop everything" to address the task at hand.

Characteristics of Urgent Tasks:

- Require immediate attention and action.
- Are deadline-driven (e.g., end-of-day reports, crisis management).
- Interrupt current work, often leading to a reactive, "firefighting" mindset.

Questions to Determine Urgency:

- "Is there a deadline for this task?"

- "If I delay this task, will it create additional problems?"
- "Is someone waiting on me to complete this task right now?"

Common Examples of Urgent Tasks:

- An urgent client complaint that could lead to loss of business.
- A last-minute request for a report due by end-of-day.
- System outages or equipment failures that disrupt workflow.

2. Importance

Importance refers to the task's impact on long-term goals, values, and success. Unlike urgency, importance is not tied to immediate deadlines. Important tasks are those that contribute to strategic outcomes and help build the foundation for future success.

Characteristics of Important Tasks:

- Contribute to long-term goals, development, or growth.
- Are proactive rather than reactive.
- Often require deep focus, planning, and strategic thinking.

Questions to Determine Importance:

- "Does this task help me achieve a long-term goal or team objective?"
- "Is this task essential to the success of a key project or deliverable?"
- "Will the impact of this task be felt weeks, months, or years from now?"

Common Examples of Important Tasks:

- Professional development, coaching, and mentoring team members
- Strategic planning, goal setting, and process improvement
- Drafting a long-term business development plan or departmental strategy.

How Urgency and Importance Interact

When urgency and importance intersect, they create four distinct categories, or quadrants, which supervisors can use to classify their tasks. Here's how these two elements intersect:

Urgency	Important	Not Important
Urgent	Quadrant I: Urgent and important	Quadrant III: Urgent but not important
Not Urgent	Quadrant II: Important but not urgent	Quadrant IV: Neither urgent nor important

Each of these quadrants plays a specific role in time management and priority setting. Let's explore them in detail.

Components of the Matrix

Quadrant I: Urgent and Important

These are the "firefighting" tasks that require immediate attention and have significant consequences if left undone. They often arise unexpectedly and demand swift, decisive action. While some of these tasks are unavoidable, excessive time spent in this quadrant can lead to stress, burnout, and a reactive management style.

Characteristics:

- Crises, emergencies, and last-minute deadlines
- Require quick decision making and action
- Cannot be delegated without risking negative consequences

Examples:

- Resolving a technical failure impacting operations
- Finalizing a report requested at the last minute by senior management
- Addressing an urgent customer complaint that could lead to a loss of business

How to Manage Quadrant I:

- Reduce reliance on this quadrant by planning ahead and anticipating risks.
- Identify recurring crises and address the root causes to prevent them in the future.
- Use contingency planning to reduce the likelihood of emergencies.

Quadrant II: Important but Not Urgent

Quadrant II represents proactive, strategic work that is essential to long-term success. Unfortunately, because these tasks lack immediate deadlines, they are often overlooked or postponed. However, investing time in this quadrant prevents quadrant I crises from arising.

Characteristics:

- Long-term, strategic initiatives
- Preventative, growth-oriented, and improvement-focused
- Require planning, preparation, and uninterrupted focus

Examples:

- Developing a team development workshop
- Building a long-term departmental strategy
- Engaging in leadership development or professional growth activities

How to Manage Quadrant II:

- Schedule time for quadrant II activities in your calendar.
- Protect this time from interruptions, as it often requires deep focus.
- Recognize that time spent here reduces the frequency of quadrant I crises.

Quadrant III: Urgent but Not Important

These are the tasks that demand immediate attention but offer little impact on long-term success. They are often interruptions caused by others' priorities, not your own. The key is to delegate or minimize time spent on these activities.

Characteristics:

- Often appear urgent due to deadlines imposed by others
- Interruptive tasks that disrupt focus and productivity
- May seem important but have little to no impact on strategic goals

Examples:

- Responding to noncritical e-mails or instant messages
- Attending unnecessary meetings
- Answering non-urgent questions from colleagues

How to Manage Quadrant III:

- Delegate tasks to team members or colleagues
- Politely decline or reschedule unnecessary meetings
- Use time blocking to handle routine communication at set times

Quadrant IV: Neither Urgent nor Important

These tasks are pure distractions. They add no value to you, your team, or your organization. Quadrant IV activities are the primary source of "time-wasting" behavior, and eliminating them is key to productivity.

Characteristics:

- Time-wasting, low-value activities
- Activities that feel "productive" but have no strategic impact
- Often pursued as a form of procrastination

Examples:

- Excessive social media scrolling
- Perfectionism on low-impact, routine tasks
- Prolonged conversations unrelated to work

How to Manage Quadrant IV:

- Eliminate or drastically reduce time spent on these activities.
- Use self-awareness to recognize when you are engaging in unproductive habits.
- Limit social media use and personal device usage during work hours.

Why the Eisenhower Matrix Matters for Supervisors

Effective time management is one of the most critical skills for supervisors, as it directly impacts productivity, team efficiency, and stress levels. The Eisenhower Matrix, also known as the Urgent-Important Matrix, provides a structured approach to prioritizing tasks based on urgency and importance. By categorizing tasks into four quadrants, supervisors can make more strategic decisions about where to focus their time and energy. Understanding how to apply this framework can help supervisors prevent burnout, encourage strategic thinking, improve decision making, and delegate effectively.

Preventing Burnout: Balancing Urgent and Important Tasks

Supervisors who spend too much time in quadrants I (urgent and important) and III (urgent but not important) often find themselves constantly firefighting—addressing last-minute crises and responding to interruptions rather than making meaningful progress on long-term goals. This reactive approach increases stress and diminishes productivity. However, by dedicating more time to quadrant II (important but not urgent), supervisors can engage in proactive planning, skill development, and relationship-building. Investing in quadrant II activities—such as employee training, strategic planning, and process improvements—reduces the frequency of crises, thereby decreasing the need for constant firefighting. This shift in focus leads to a healthier work–life balance and a more sustainable management style.

Encouraging Strategic Thinking: Prioritizing Quadrant II Tasks

Many supervisors struggle to move beyond daily operational tasks to focus on strategic initiatives. The Eisenhower Matrix emphasizes the importance of quadrant II, where tasks related to growth, team development, and long-term planning reside. By prioritizing these activities, supervisors can drive meaningful progress within their teams and organizations. For example, instead of only reacting to immediate performance issues, a supervisor who invests time in quadrant II might implement a mentorship program, create a structured training curriculum, or refine workflow processes. These efforts yield long-term benefits by developing employees' skills, improving team efficiency, and preventing recurring problems that would otherwise demand urgent attention later.

Improving Decision Making: Recognizing What Deserves Attention

Supervisors often face an overwhelming number of tasks and responsibilities, making it difficult to determine which activities deserve priority. The Eisenhower Matrix simplifies this process by clarifying which tasks should be addressed immediately, scheduled for later, delegated, or eliminated. Quadrant I tasks require immediate attention, but supervisors must be cautious about mistaking quadrant III tasks (urgent but not important) for priorities. Many interruptions, unnecessary meetings, and minor administrative tasks fall into quadrant III, consuming valuable time without yielding significant results. By recognizing these distractions, supervisors can make better-informed decisions about where to invest their time, ensuring that high-impact tasks receive the attention they deserve.

Empowering Delegation: Shifting Quadrant III Tasks to the Team

One of the most powerful insights the Eisenhower Matrix provides is the ability to distinguish tasks that can—and should—be delegated. Quadrant III consists of tasks that are urgent but not important, meaning they demand immediate attention but do not necessarily require the supervisor's expertise. These tasks, such as scheduling meetings, responding to noncritical e-mails, or handling routine approvals, can often be assigned to team members. Delegation not only frees up a supervisor's time for higher-value work but also empowers employees by providing them with opportunities for growth and decision making. When supervisors use the Eisenhower Matrix to assess their workload, they can confidently assign appropriate tasks to their team, fostering a culture of trust and efficiency.

By applying the principles of the Eisenhower Matrix, supervisors can transition from reactive management to a more proactive and strategic leadership style. Prioritizing quadrant II tasks leads to long-term improvements, reduces the frequency of crises, and ensures that time is spent on activities that create the greatest impact. Through better decision making and effective delegation, supervisors can enhance both their productivity and the overall performance of their teams.

Balancing Team Priorities

Supervisors are responsible not only for managing their own time effectively but also for guiding their teams in prioritizing tasks to maximize productivity. A well-balanced team operates efficiently, meets deadlines without excessive stress, and focuses on high-impact activities that align with organizational goals. Achieving this balance requires a clear understanding of team tasks, effective delegation, the ability to deprioritize or eliminate low-value tasks, and strategies to manage conflicts and competing priorities.

Understanding Team Tasks

To effectively balance team priorities, supervisors must first gain a comprehensive understanding of their team's workload and key responsibilities. Regular check-ins with team members provide insights into ongoing projects, upcoming deadlines, and potential roadblocks. By asking questions such as, "What is your priority task this week?" and "Which deadlines are critical, and which can be adjusted?", supervisors can identify bottlenecks and ensure that the most pressing tasks are addressed efficiently. These discussions help create a shared understanding of team objectives and allow supervisors to provide guidance on workload distribution.

Effective Delegation

Delegation is a key component of time management and team efficiency. While this topic will be explored in greater detail in the next chapter, it is important to recognize that supervisors should assign tasks based on team members' strengths, experience, and development goals. Research from the Center for Creative Leadership highlights that effective delegation not only improves team dynamics but also enhances skill development, leading to higher job satisfaction and stronger engagement. Supervisors who delegate appropriately free up their own time for strategic decision making while simultaneously empowering their employees to take ownership of key responsibilities.

Identifying Tasks to Deprioritize or Eliminate

Not all tasks contribute equally to organizational success, and part of balancing team priorities involves recognizing which tasks can be deprioritized or eliminated altogether. Supervisors should encourage their teams to reflect on the value of their work and determine whether certain processes are necessary or could be streamlined. For example, if routine reports do not provide actionable insights, the process may need to be revised or removed. Similarly, time-consuming administrative tasks that add little value should be reassessed. By continuously evaluating the relevance of tasks, supervisors ensure that their teams focus on high-impact work rather than getting bogged down by low-priority activities.

Managing Conflicts and Competing Priorities

In any team, conflicts and competing priorities will inevitably arise. Supervisors play a critical role in helping their teams navigate these challenges by fostering open communication and facilitating discussions to realign priorities. Transparent conversations about shifting deadlines, resource constraints, and evolving business needs ensure that everyone understands how their work contributes to the overall team and organizational success. By providing clarity and involving employees in decision making, supervisors promote collaboration and reduce friction among team members. Encouraging adaptability and reinforcing the importance of shared goals enables teams to handle competing priorities with confidence and efficiency.

Balancing team priorities is an ongoing process that requires communication, flexibility, and strategic decision making. By understanding workloads, delegating effectively, eliminating unnecessary tasks, and proactively managing conflicts, supervisors can create a work environment where employees feel empowered, focused, and productive. With a structured approach to prioritization, teams can achieve their goals while maintaining a healthy and sustainable workflow.

Implications for Supervisors

Effectively balancing team priorities has significant benefits for both individual employees and the organization as a whole. A well-structured approach to prioritization enhances team morale, increases productivity, and reduces stress by preventing unnecessary work overload. When supervisors foster a culture of strategic time management, teams operate with greater cohesion and clarity.

A collaborative approach to prioritization also strengthens team communication and accountability. When employees understand how their tasks contribute to broader organizational goals, they take greater ownership of their work and feel empowered to make informed decisions. However, supervisors must also navigate challenges such as conflicting priorities and resistance to process changes. Addressing these challenges requires patience, adaptability, and transparency.

For example, in a busy office where multiple team members face overlapping deadlines, a supervisor can host a team meeting to openly discuss workloads, redistribute tasks, and set clear priorities. This proactive approach ensures that resources are allocated effectively, reducing stress and promoting a more balanced workflow. By consistently applying these strategies, supervisors can create a productive work environment that encourages focus, efficiency, and long-term success.

Case Study: A New Supervisor's Time Management Journey

When Maria was promoted to Project Manager at TechFlow Solutions, she faced a challenge common to many new supervisors: managing the launch of a critical new software platform while transitioning from a star performer to team leader. With a team of six developers, a tight 8-week timeline, and responsibility for a $2 million project, she needed to quickly master both time management and delegation.

The Initial Challenge

In her first week, Maria found herself:

- Responding to 100+ daily e-mails
- Attending 6 to 7 hours of meetings daily
- Still coding alongside her team
- Struggling to find time for strategic planning
- Dealing with constant interruptions

"I was working longer hours but accomplishing less," Maria recalled. "I knew something had to change."

Implementing the Eisenhower Matrix

Maria began by categorizing all tasks using the Eisenhower Matrix: Urgent and Important:

- Critical bug fixes affecting current clients
- Key client meetings
- Immediate team blockers

Important but not urgent:

- Strategic platform development planning
- Team member development conversations
- Process improvement initiatives

Urgent but not important:

- Most e-mail responses
- Status update requests
- Routine meetings

Neither urgent nor important:

- General office discussions
- Noncritical system notifications
- Routine code reviews (could be delegated)

Making Strategic Changes

Based on this analysis, Maria implemented several changes:

1. Time Blocking
   - Reserved 8 to 10 a.m. for strategic work
   - Scheduled e-mail checking for specific times
   - Created "office hours" for team questions
2. Delegation Strategy
   - Assigned senior developers as technical leads
   - Created rotation for routine code reviews
   - Empowered team members to make specific decisions
3. Meeting Management
   - Reduced 1-hour meetings to 30 minutes
   - Implemented "no-meeting Wednesdays"
   - Required agendas for all meetings

Results After 2 Months

The impact was significant:

- Project launched on schedule
- Team productivity increased by 35 percent
- Maria's working hours decreased from 60 to 45 weekly
- Employee satisfaction scores improved by 40 percent
- Critical strategic initiatives progressed faster

Key Lessons for New Supervisors

1. Prioritization is Personal
   What's urgent for others isn't necessarily urgent for you. Maria
   learned to evaluate requests based on team and project impact.
2. Time Blocking Works
   Protecting time for important but non-urgent tasks is essential
   for long-term success.
3. Delegation is Critical
   Success comes through enabling others rather than doing everything yourself.

Team Member Perspective

"Initially, we were concerned when Maria stopped being as immediately
available," said David, a senior developer. "But her new structure actually helped us become more self-sufficient and productive. We learned to
solve many issues ourselves and grew as professionals."

Conclusion: Mastering Time and Priorities— A Supervisor's Critical Challenge

The journey from individual contributor to successful supervisor hinges
on your ability to manage both time and priorities effectively. As we've
seen throughout this chapter, this transition requires more than just better scheduling—it demands a fundamental shift in how you view and
invest your time.

When supervisors effectively manage their time and set clear expectations, teams thrive. While specific metrics may vary across studies,
research consistently affirms the connection between strong supervisory time management and improved outcomes in team performance,
employee satisfaction, and resource utilization. Gallup's findings show
that managers play a defining role in engagement and productivity, and
McKinsey research highlights how poor prioritization often undermines
a team's ability to perform at its highest potential. Ultimately, mastering

time as a supervisor is not just about efficiency—it's about unlocking your team's collective potential.

The Eisenhower Matrix provides a crucial framework for this transition, helping you distinguish between what's truly important and merely urgent. Success comes not from handling every crisis, but from investing time in quadrant II activities that prevent crises from occurring. As one experienced supervisor noted, "The best time management strategy is crisis prevention through proper planning."

Key Principles to Remember

First, prioritization is about choices. Every "yes" to an urgent but unimportant task is a "no" to strategic thinking and team development. Make these choices consciously. Second, time management and expectation-setting are inseparable. Clear expectations create efficiency, reduce confusion, and enable better prioritization for everyone on your team. Third, success isn't measured by how busy you are, but by how effectively you invest your time in activities that drive results. Focus on what matters most—strategic planning, team development, and proactive problem solving.

Looking ahead, one of the most powerful tools for effective time management is delegation. In the next chapter, we'll explore how to delegate effectively, enabling you to focus on strategic priorities while developing your team's capabilities and confidence. But first, complete those worksheets!

Remember: Time is your most precious resource as a supervisor. How you choose to invest it will determine not just your success, but your team's ability to achieve its full potential.

Your path to becoming an exceptional supervisor starts with mastering your time.

CHAPTER 5

Delegating Effectively

Effective delegation is like planting seeds in a garden. It takes trust, patience, and care, but when done right, it yields a vibrant, flourishing team.

The Art of Letting Go: Mastering Effective Delegation

When I first stepped into a supervisory role, a colleague shared what seemed like cold advice: "If it's something my team can do, I don't touch it." Initially, this struck me as detached leadership. Over time, however, I came to recognize it as one of the most profound insights into effective supervision.

Effective delegation is a cornerstone of successful leadership. When managers delegate well, they free themselves to focus on strategic priorities while giving team members opportunities to grow. Despite the clear benefits, many leaders still spend large portions of their time on tasks that could easily be handled by others. This not only leads to unnecessary workload and burnout but also deprives employees of valuable chances to build skills and take ownership. Delegation, when done intentionally, boosts team productivity, increases efficiency, and fosters trust. It's not just about offloading tasks—it's about empowering others, strengthening the team, and creating a more agile and effective organization.

The Evolution of Leadership

Consider how organizations grow: They often start with a small group handling everything, much like a startup with founders wearing multiple hats. As demands increase and teams expand, success depends on the ability to shift from "doing everything" to "enabling others to succeed." This transition isn't unique to startups—it's the fundamental journey every supervisor must navigate.

This shift from "doer" to "enabler" represents what Watkins (2012) calls the "seven seismic shifts" leaders must make as they advance. One of the most important—and most difficult—of these shifts is mastering the art of delegation. In my experience, successful delegation depends on four core practices: clearly defining boundaries of authority, matching tasks to individual strengths, using delegation as a developmental tool, and offering support without micromanaging. These align closely with what Covey (1989) called "stewardship delegation," a mindset that emphasizes responsibility for results rather than rigid adherence to methods. When supervisors apply these principles, I've consistently seen improvements in team problem-solving, job satisfaction, and overall performance. Delegation, in this light, becomes more than a time-management tactic—it's a foundational leadership discipline that expands capacity and builds resilience.

The Science Behind Successful Delegation

Research from Bohns and Flynn (2021) at Cornell University's Organizational Behavior Department reveals why some supervisors excel at delegation while others struggle. Their findings show that successful delegation isn't just about assigning tasks—it's about creating a system that measures and promotes:

- Task completion rate: Both speed and quality of delegated work
- Employee growth: Skill development through new responsibilities
- Team capacity: Overall increase in capabilities
- Supervisor focus: Time freed for strategic activities

Rozovsky and Hoffman's (2019) study of Google's implementation of these principles in their engineering teams demonstrates the power of systematic delegation, resulting in 40 percent faster project completion, 55 percent increase in innovation initiatives, and 38 percent improvement in team satisfaction.

The Real Challenge

If you've ever felt the pull to "just do it yourself" because it's faster or easier, you're not alone. Many first-time supervisors struggle with letting go, worried that others might not meet their standards or that explaining tasks takes too much time. However, effective supervisors understand that their role isn't about doing the work—it's about building a team capable of exceeding expectations.

Let's learn how to transform delegation from a task-shifting exercise into a powerful tool for team development and organizational growth.

Remember: Every time you choose not to delegate an appropriate task, you're choosing not to invest in your team's growth. Let's explore how to make those investments wisely and effectively.

How does delegation benefit you and the team?

Empowers Team Members

When supervisors delegate tasks to their team members, they provide an opportunity for those employees to take ownership of their work. Delegation shows employees that their contributions are valued and trusted, which increases motivation and engagement.

How It Works:

- Control shifts to ownership: When employees have full responsibility for a task, they are more likely to take it seriously. They begin to see the impact of their efforts on the larger goals of the team or organization.
- Confidence grows: Each successfully delegated task builds employee confidence. When they see they can rise to the challenge, they are more willing to take on greater responsibility in the future.

Example:

A supervisor overseeing a marketing team assigns the development of a social media strategy to a junior team member with an interest in social media analytics. By allowing them to create and present the strategy to senior leadership, the team member builds confidence in their ability to lead future projects.

Promotes Employee Development

Delegation is one of the most effective ways to develop employee skills and prepare them for future roles. When employees are given "stretch assignments"—tasks that challenge them beyond their usual responsibilities—they are forced to learn, adapt, and grow.

How It Works:

- New skills are acquired: Employees gain technical and interpersonal skills they wouldn't have developed if they'd stayed within the confines of their original role.
- Succession planning: When supervisors delegate key responsibilities, they're building a pipeline of future leaders. Team members who grow their capabilities are more likely to be considered for promotions or larger roles within the organization.

Example:

An operations manager assigns a team member the task of leading the department's annual budgeting process—something the manager had always done themselves. While the employee initially feels overwhelmed, they gain valuable skills in financial analysis, forecasting, and stakeholder communication.

Frees Up the Supervisor's Time for Strategic Work

Many supervisors become overwhelmed with "busy work"—administrative tasks, routine check-ins, and repetitive reporting. While these tasks are important, they don't require the unique perspective of a supervisor. By delegating these tasks, supervisors free themselves to focus on high-impact strategic work, such as planning, problem solving, and innovation.

How It Works:

- Less time in the weeds, more time on strategy: Supervisors can shift their attention from "small tasks" to "big-picture thinking," such as process improvements, growth initiatives, and higher-level planning.

- Capacity to lead: Without delegation, supervisors are trapped in an endless loop of task completion. Delegation allows them to lead, coach, and make strategic decisions.

Example:

A supervisor in a logistics company delegates the responsibility for tracking incoming shipments to a team lead. With this task off their plate, the supervisor can focus on re-engineering the warehouse's layout to improve efficiency—a strategic initiative with a much larger impact on the company's bottom line.

Increases Team Accountability

Delegation shifts accountability from the supervisor to the employee. When team members are responsible for key deliverables, they become more invested in the process and the outcome. This accountability increases motivation and encourages self-direction.

How It Works:

- Ownership culture: Instead of feeling like they're simply "doing what they're told," employees feel like they "own" specific outcomes, which leads to a stronger sense of purpose.
- Peer-to-peer accountability: When one team member is clearly assigned a task, their peers know who to go to for questions or assistance. This clarity reduces confusion and finger-pointing.

Example:

A supervisor of a customer service team assigns one team member to manage the monthly customer feedback survey. This responsibility gives the employee a sense of ownership over the task. Instead of waiting for the supervisor to follow up, the employee takes the initiative to complete the survey, analyze the data, and present actionable insights to the team.

Enhances Team Engagement and Morale

When employees are given more responsibility and autonomy, they feel more engaged in their work. People want to feel that their contributions matter. Delegation signals to employees that their skills are valued and that their role is essential to the team's success.

How It Works:

- Increased job satisfaction: Employees feel more fulfilled when they know their work directly contributes to important outcomes.
- Sense of purpose: Employees who are trusted with meaningful work feel a stronger connection to the company's mission and values.

Example:

An HR supervisor allows team members to lead monthly onboarding sessions for new hires. Team members feel more involved in the company's growth and development, increasing job satisfaction and team morale.

Supports Team Flexibility and Resilience

If one person holds all the knowledge and tasks, the team becomes dependent on that person. But if responsibilities are shared through delegation, the team becomes more flexible and resilient.

How It Works:

- Cross-training happens naturally: As tasks are shared across the team, employees learn how to perform roles beyond their own. This increases team adaptability.
- Less disruption during absences: If an employee or supervisor is out for a week, someone else can step in and maintain business continuity.

Example:

A software development team rotates responsibility for "bug triage" each week, ensuring that everyone on the team knows how to identify, prioritize, and resolve software issues. This practice builds team-wide resilience, especially during times of employee absence or turnover.

Creates a Path for Team Growth

Delegation doesn't just make current processes smoother—it lays the foundation for future growth. When supervisors develop the capacity of their team, they create opportunities for scaling operations, promoting employees, and preparing for larger goals.

How It Works:

- Room for promotion: Employees who successfully take on delegated tasks become prime candidates for promotion, allowing the organization to "hire from within."
- Operational scalability: When multiple people know how to perform essential tasks, the team is ready to take on larger projects or higher workloads.

Example:

A finance supervisor trains a team member to manage end-of-month reporting. Over time, that team member becomes so skilled at the task that they are promoted to an analyst role. Meanwhile, the supervisor focuses on automation tools to improve the efficiency of future reports.

Why Supervisors Fail to Delegate

If delegation is so beneficial, why do so many supervisors fail to do it? Here are the most common reasons:

- "I Can Do It Faster Myself": Yes, it may be faster in the short term, but it's inefficient in the long term.
- "I Don't Trust My Team": This reflects a lack of training, clarity, or control. Supervisors must train employees to build trust.
- "I Don't Want to Let Go": Some supervisors derive self-worth from being "the go-to person." Delegation requires a shift in mindset from "doing" to "leading."

The Bottom Line

Delegation is not just a convenience—it's a leadership necessity. It empowers employees, supports professional development, increases productivity, and allows supervisors to focus on high-impact work. Supervisors who fail to delegate risk burnout, employee disengagement, and team stagnation. But those who master delegation build more capable teams, reduce their own stress, and position themselves as leaders ready to take on larger roles.

So, ask yourself: *Are you holding on to tasks you should be letting go of?* If the answer is yes, this chapter will show you how to identify those tasks, build the trust required to delegate, and follow proven strategies to ensure success. By the end of this chapter, you'll have the confidence to let go—and when you do, you'll discover just how powerful your team can be.

Effective Delegation Techniques

Mastering delegation requires more than handing out tasks—it involves thoughtful planning, clear communication, and ongoing support. The following techniques will help you delegate more effectively, ensuring both you and your team achieve success.

Match Tasks to Team Members' Strengths and Interests

"The right person for the right task."

Why It Matters:

Delegation is most successful when tasks are aligned with the strengths, skills, and interests of your team members. When employees feel a sense of purpose and connection to their assignments, they're more engaged, motivated, and likely to produce high-quality results.

How to Do It:

- Assess skills and interests: During one-on-one meetings or performance reviews, ask employees about their career goals and personal interests. Use this information when assigning tasks.

- Use a skills matrix: Create a simple table listing each employee and their skills. This allows you to see who is best suited for specific tasks.
- Start small: If you're unsure about a person's ability, assign a small, manageable task as a trial.

Example:

A finance manager knows that one team member enjoys working with spreadsheets and data analysis. When it's time to prepare a quarterly financial report, the manager assigns this task to that team member, ensuring better performance and higher engagement.

Pro Tip: People are more engaged when their assignments are connected to their long-term goals. Ask team members where they'd like to grow and delegate tasks that align with those aspirations.

Set Clear Expectations

"Ambiguity breeds confusion, but clarity breeds results."

Why It Matters:

If your team doesn't know what success looks like, they'll struggle to meet your expectations. Clarity on deliverables, deadlines, and decision-making authority is essential to effective delegation.

How to Do It:

- Define the "What, When, and How": What needs to be done? By when? How should it be done? Answer these questions clearly.
- Use SMART goals: Make sure your tasks are specific, measurable, achievable, relevant, and time-bound.
- Put it in writing: Document expectations in e-mails, project management tools, or shared documents so team members have a point of reference.

Example:

Instead of saying, *"Please put together a client report for Friday,"* say, *"Please create a 5-page client report that includes a summary of Q3 performance, customer feedback, and recommendations for next steps. Submit it to me by 3 PM on Friday."*

Pro Tip: Ask team members to repeat back what they've heard. This ensures they understand the scope, expectations, and timeline of the task.

Provide the Right Amount of Guidance and Support

"Don't give them a fish, but don't throw them in the ocean without a life vest either."

Why It Matters:

Delegating isn't about abandoning your team—it's about supporting them without taking over. Too much guidance leads to micromanagement, while too little leaves employees feeling lost.

How to Do It:

- Assess skill levels: For experienced employees, provide high-level guidance. For less experienced employees, be more hands-on.
- Provide resources: Ensure employees have access to the tools, templates, training, and contacts they need to complete the task.
- Check in without hovering: Schedule check-ins at key milestones but avoid daily status updates unless necessary.

Example:

A project manager delegates a presentation to a team member. Instead of hovering, the manager sets a check-in meeting for mid-week to review progress and offer feedback. The team member feels supported but still has autonomy.

Pro Tip: Early in the task, schedule one check-in to discuss progress. Toward the end of the task, reduce check-ins to prevent micromanagement.

Grant Authority, Not Just Responsibility

"If they can't make decisions, they aren't truly in charge."

Why It Matters:

Assigning responsibility without giving employees the authority to make decisions creates frustration and delays. True delegation means letting go of some control and trusting your team to make decisions within a defined scope.

How to Do It:

- Clarify decision-making authority: Be clear on what decisions they can make and what needs your approval.
- Establish boundaries: Define the limits of their decision-making power. For example, "You can approve expenses up to $500."
- Avoid overruling decisions: If you give them authority, respect their choices—even if you would have done it differently.

Example:

An HR supervisor delegates the responsibility of scheduling interviews to a junior HR assistant. The assistant is also given authority to choose time slots and communicate directly with candidates, which speeds up the process and builds the assistant's confidence.

Pro Tip: If you delegate responsibility but retain all decision-making power, you're not delegating—you're just outsourcing the labor.

Avoid Micromanaging

"Don't look over their shoulder; let them take the lead."

Why It Matters:

If you micromanage, your team will become dependent on you, and you'll never free yourself from the daily grind. True delegation requires trust, patience, and the ability to step back.

How to Do It:

- Delegate the outcome, not the method: Let them decide *how* to achieve the goal.
- Provide feedback, not control: Offer constructive feedback after the task is complete, not during every step.
- Resist the urge to "check in constantly": Use project management tools to track progress without hovering.

Example:

A marketing manager assigns a team member to design a new social media campaign. Instead of telling them which colors, fonts, and images to use, the manager defines the goal: *"Create a campaign that increases clicks by 20%."* This allows for creative freedom.

Pro Tip: Ask yourself, *"Am I delegating or am I directing?"* If you're telling them exactly how to do every step, you're directing, not delegating.

Ensure Accountability

"What gets tracked gets done."

Why It Matters:

When team members know they'll be held accountable, they take ownership of the task. Accountability creates urgency, promotes follow-through, and increases the likelihood of success.

How to Do It:

- Set deadlines: Every task should have a clear due date, even if it's part of a larger project.
- Use tracking tools: Tools like Trello, Asana, or Microsoft Teams keep everyone on the same page.
- Hold debrief meetings: Once the task is complete, hold a review session to discuss successes and areas for improvement.

Example:

A supervisor asks a team member to lead the quarterly sales review presentation. They set a deadline, track progress through a shared checklist, and schedule a debrief session to review what went well and what could improve.

Pro Tip: If you don't follow up, employees will think the task wasn't important. When you check in, it signals that their work matters.

Start Small and Build Trust

"Small wins lead to big results."

Why It Matters:

If you're hesitant to delegate big responsibilities, start small. Assign smaller, low-risk tasks and build trust over time. This allows you to observe your team's skills and identify who is ready for bigger roles.

How to Do It:

- Start with low-risk tasks: Assign small administrative tasks, daily reports, or coordination duties first.
- Gradually increase responsibility: As employees succeed, give them more autonomy and larger tasks.
- Acknowledge progress: Celebrate their success and reinforce their growth.

Example:

A new supervisor assigns a team member the task of organizing meeting agendas and following up with attendees. As the team member shows proficiency, they're later given the responsibility of running team meetings.

Pro Tip: View delegation as a "test-and-learn" process. Start with small wins to build confidence for bigger responsibilities.

Close the Loop with Feedback

"Feedback isn't the end—it's the beginning of the next task."

Why It Matters:

Feedback transforms delegation into a learning experience. Without feedback, employees won't know if they succeeded or where they can improve.

How to Do It:

- Give specific feedback: Use the "SBI" (situation, behavior, impact) model to make feedback clear.
- Provide praise and growth opportunities: Acknowledge successes and identify areas for improvement.

Example:

After a team member leads a client meeting, the supervisor offers feedback: *"You handled the client's objections well (behavior), which built trust (impact). Next time, let's prepare for potential objections in advance (growth opportunity)."*

Pro Tip: Always "close the loop" by providing clear, actionable feedback using the SBI (situation, behavior, impact) model. Celebrate successes, highlight areas for growth, and set the stage for continuous improvement. This approach turns every task into a learning opportunity.

Case Study: Transforming Team Performance Through Delegation

The Challenge

When Elena Rodriguez was promoted to Development Team Lead at Quantum Software Solutions, she inherited a struggling team of six developers with missed deadlines, low morale, and a reputation for inconsistent quality. As a former star developer herself, her instinct was to dive in and fix everything personally.

"I was working 70-hour weeks trying to review every line of code, attend every meeting, and solve every problem," Elena recalls. "I was exhausted, my team felt micromanaged, and we were still missing deadlines."

The Breaking Point

Three months into her role, a critical client project fell behind schedule. The VP of Engineering asked Elena a question that changed her approach: "Are you building a team or just doing the work of six people?"

The Delegation Framework
Elena implemented a structured approach to delegation:

1. Skills assessment: First, she conducted detailed one-on-one meetings with each team member, focusing on:
   - Technical strengths and interests
   - Career aspirations
   - Areas for development
   - Current confidence levels
2. Task analysis and assignment: Elena created a responsibility matrix that:
   - Matched tasks with team member strengths
   - Identified growth opportunities
   - Clearly defined authority levels
   - Established success metrics
3. Clear handoff process: For each delegated task, Elena ensured:
   - Written documentation of expectations
   - Defined check-in points
   - Clear success criteria
   - Specified decision-making authority

Practical Example: The Authentication System Update

Previously, Elena would have handled this critical project herself. Instead, she:

1. Delegated project lead role to Maya, a motivated mid-level developer
2. Established clear parameters:
   - Final architecture review required
   - Authority to make routine decisions
   - Weekly progress updates
   - Specific performance metrics
3. Provided support through:
   - Regular but brief check-ins
   - Available for questions during set office hours
   - Technical guidance without taking over

The Results

After 6 months of implementing this delegation framework:

- Team velocity increased by 40 percent
- Code quality metrics improved by 35 percent
- Employee satisfaction scores rose from 65 to 89 percent
- Elena's working hours reduced to 45 per week
- Two team members were promoted based on demonstrated growth

Maya's Perspective

> Being trusted with the authentication project was a turning point for me. Elena made her expectations clear but gave me room to solve problems my way. When I struggled, she guided me without taking over. I learned more in those 3 months than in my previous year.

Key Lessons for New Supervisors

1. Start small—begin with lower-risk tasks to build trust and confidence on both sides.
2. Be clear about authority—explicitly state what decisions team members can make independently.
3. Create safety nets—establish check-in points that allow for course correction without micromanagement.
4. Focus on growth—use delegation as a development tool, matching tasks to development goals.
5. Document and track—maintain clear records of delegated tasks, expectations, and outcomes.

The Transformation

"The hardest part wasn't learning to delegate—it was unlearning the habit of doing everything myself," Elena reflects. "Once I truly embraced delegation as a development tool rather than just task assignment, everything changed. My team grew stronger, our work improved, and I finally had time to think strategically about our future."

Mastering Delegation for Success

Delegation isn't just a management technique—it's a leadership necessity. It's the difference between being a task-driven doer and a strategic leader. The most effective supervisors recognize that their value isn't measured by how much they accomplish alone but by how much their team achieves together. Mastering delegation empowers employees, enhances productivity, and allows supervisors to focus on strategic initiatives that drive lasting impact.

Delegation isn't easy. It requires trust, patience, and a shift in mindset. Many first-time supervisors struggle with letting go. They worry their team won't meet expectations, fear that delegation will backfire, or believe it's just easier to "do it themselves." But this mindset is a trap. By clinging to tasks, supervisors not only risk burnout but also stifle the growth of their team.

On the flip side, supervisors who master delegation free themselves to think bigger, lead with clarity, and build a team that thrives on ownership, accountability, and autonomy. The process is more than just handing off assignments—it's about empowering employees, nurturing their development, and creating a resilient, future-ready team.

What Great Delegation Looks Like

Great delegation isn't random—it's intentional and thoughtful. It starts with knowing your team. Who has the skills, interests, and capacity to take on new challenges? From there, supervisors set clear expectations, grant both responsibility and authority, and support their team with just the right amount of guidance. Along the way, supervisors track progress, hold team members accountable, and close the loop with constructive feedback.

When done correctly, delegation benefits everyone:

- Supervisors free themselves to lead: Instead of getting stuck in the day-to-day grind, they can focus on strategic work, such as process improvements, team development, and long-term planning.

- Team members grow their skills and confidence: As they tackle more challenging tasks, employees gain new skills, feel more engaged, and build the confidence to take on larger roles.
- The organization becomes more resilient: When knowledge and responsibility are distributed across the team, the organization is less vulnerable to absences, turnover, or disruptions.

Conclusion: Key Takeaways for Effective Delegation

If there's one essential truth about delegation, it's this: Delegation is not about letting go—it's about lifting others up. Effective delegation is a leadership skill that enables supervisors to develop their teams, increase efficiency, and create a culture of trust and empowerment. The strongest supervisors delegate not to offload work, but to create opportunities for their employees to grow and succeed.

Here are the core principles of effective delegation:

1. **Match the task to the right person**—Align tasks with individual strengths, skills, and career aspirations. Employees who see purpose in their work are more engaged and perform at a higher level.
2. **Set clear expectations**—Clearly define what needs to be done, the deadline, and the standard of quality expected. Unclear direction leads to confusion and subpar results.
3. **Provide the right support**—Offer the necessary tools, resources, and initial guidance, and then step back. Let team members take ownership and find their own solutions.
4. **Grant authority, not just responsibility**—Delegation only works when employees have the autonomy to make decisions. Assigning tasks without granting authority leads to frustration and inefficiency.
5. **Trust, don't micromanage**—Supervisors must resist the urge to take back control. Once a task is delegated, allow the employee to take full ownership while providing support when needed.

6. **Hold team members accountable**—Establish check-in points, track progress, and ensure follow-through. Accountability fosters a sense of ownership and keeps projects on track.

7. **Provide feedback and recognize success**—Effective delegation is a cycle of learning and improvement. Recognizing achievements and offering constructive feedback helps employees refine their skills and confidence.

How to Apply These Lessons

Mastering delegation doesn't happen overnight. Start small. Identify one task you currently handle that could be delegated. Choose the right team member, provide clear guidance, and allow them the space to succeed. As you refine your approach, delegation will become a natural and essential part of your leadership style.

Supervisors who delegate effectively experience a profound shift in their work dynamic:

- *Less stress*—You are no longer carrying every task alone.
- *Stronger teams*—Employees develop confidence, skills, and self-sufficiency.
- *More strategic leadership*—Delegation frees up mental space for big-picture thinking and planning.

A Final Word on Delegation

Consider what a previous supervisor once said to me: *"If it's something my team can do, I don't touch it."* At first, this seemed dismissive. But in reality, it was a profound statement of trust, empowerment, and leadership. Supervisors who try to do everything themselves limit not only their own effectiveness but also their team's potential.

This lesson is evident in successful organizations. Startups, for example, begin with founders who wear multiple hats, but they only scale by hiring, trusting, and delegating. The same is true for supervisors. Moving from *doing* to *leading* is a critical shift—and delegation is the bridge to making that transition successfully.

As you move forward, reflect on these questions:

- Am I holding on to tasks that my team could handle?
- Am I creating opportunities for my team to grow through delegation?
- Am I fostering a culture of accountability and ownership?

Mastering delegation requires patience, practice, and trust. But the rewards are undeniable. When done effectively, delegation doesn't just lighten your workload—it strengthens your team, builds capacity, and transforms you from a task manager into a true leader.

Your challenge for this week: Choose one task to delegate. Whether big or small, use the strategies outlined in this chapter to set clear expectations, empower your team, and observe the results. You may be surprised at just how ready your team is to rise to the occasion.

CHAPTER 6

Resolving Conflicts and Handling Difficult Conversations

Conflict is like a fire—it can warm your team and bring them to-gether, or it can burn bridges. It all depends on how you handle it.

The most successful supervisors understand a fundamental truth about leadership: conflict in the workplace is as natural as change itself. Like a swift current beneath still waters, tension and disagreement flow through every organization, team, and relationship. The impact of these under-currents is significant: a landmark study by CPP Inc. (2008) revealed that U.S. employees spend on average 2.8 hours per week dealing with conflict, translating to approximately $359 billion in paid hours annually.

While specific percentages may vary, research consistently indicates that a substantial portion of workplace conflicts stem from unclear expectations and poor communication—challenges that fall squarely within a supervisor's sphere of influence. For new supervisors, this presents both a challenge and an opportunity. While many enter their roles believing their primary mission is to maintain constant harmony, viewing conflict as a sign of failure, research tells a different story.

Studies by Amy Edmondson and Diana Smith (2006) suggest that when teams engage in open dialogue and challenge assumptions, they enhance their collective understanding, leading to improved performance.

Recent studies demonstrate that teams who effectively manage conflict show significant benefits. According to Behfar, Peterson, Mannix, and Trochim (2022), teams with productive conflict resolution strategies demonstrate 27 percent higher innovation rates and 29 percent stronger problem-solving capabilities. Edmondson and Dillon's research (2023) further shows that such teams develop 33 percent better long-term working relationships over time.

Think of conflict like fire—it can either warm your team and bring them together, or it can burn bridges. The difference lies not in the presence of conflict, but in how you handle it. De Dreu and Weingart's meta-analysis (2021) shows that supervisors who approach conflict with the right tools and mindset transform these challenging moments into catalysts for:

- Deeper team trust
- Enhanced collaboration
- Improved decision making
- Stronger organizational culture

Yet for many new supervisors, the prospect of addressing conflict triggers anxiety. You might feel your stomach tighten at the thought of confrontation, worry about saying the wrong thing, or fear damaging relationships. These concerns are natural—research from VitalSmarts (now Crucial Learning) found that 70 percent of managers report feeling uncomfortable when addressing problematic employee behaviors (Maxfield et al. 2013). A survey by the Society for Human Resource Management similarly revealed that 72 percent of managers avoid difficult conversations with employees, despite recognizing their importance (SHRM 2019).

This chapter will provide you with research-backed frameworks, practical tools, and proven strategies to transform difficult conversations from moments of anxiety into opportunities for positive change. You'll learn:

- How to identify and address conflict early
- Techniques for conducting challenging conversations
- Strategies for turning disagreement into productive dialogue
- Methods for building stronger relationships through conflict resolution

Remember: The goal isn't to eliminate conflict but to harness its potential for positive change. As a mentor once shared with me, "The quality of your leadership isn't measured by the absence of conflict, but by how effectively you help your team navigate through it."

Understanding the Anatomy of Workplace Conflict

Before you can effectively resolve conflicts, you need to understand their nature. Like a doctor diagnosing an illness, your ability to identify the type of conflict you're dealing with will guide your approach to resolution. Three primary types of conflict emerge in most workplace settings, each requiring its own distinct treatment.

Interpersonal Conflict: The Human Element

Maria and James work in your marketing department. Maria is methodical, detail-oriented, and likes to plan everything weeks in advance. James is creative, spontaneous, and often produces his best work under tight deadlines. While both are talented professionals, their different working styles have created increasing tension. Maria feels James's last-minute approach creates unnecessary stress, while James believes Maria's rigid planning stifles creativity.

This scenario illustrates interpersonal conflict—perhaps the most common and complex type of workplace tension. These conflicts arise from differences in personality, working styles, values, or communication preferences. They're often emotional in nature and can feel deeply personal to those involved.

What makes interpersonal conflicts particularly challenging is their tendency to spiral. What begins as a simple disagreement about work styles can evolve into personal resentment, leading to reduced collaboration, decreased productivity, and a toxic team environment. The key to managing these conflicts lies in recognizing that differences in working styles and perspectives aren't inherently problematic—they only become issues when we fail to understand and accommodate them.

Task-Related Conflict: When the "What" and "How" Collide

Your development team is launching a new product. Half the team believes in releasing early and iterating based on customer feedback. The other half argues for extensive testing to ensure a polished launch. Neither approach is wrong, but the disagreement is causing delays and frustration.

This exemplifies task-related conflict—disagreements about how work should be done, when it should be completed, or who should be responsible. Unlike interpersonal conflicts, task-related conflicts tend to be more objective and focused on the work itself rather than personalities or emotions.

These conflicts can actually be beneficial when managed properly. They often lead to better decision making as teams are forced to examine problems from multiple angles. However, if left unaddressed, task-related conflicts can evolve into interpersonal conflicts as people become emotionally invested in their preferred approaches.

Organizational Conflict: The System-Level Challenge

Your company announces a shift to a hybrid work model. Some departments interpret this as allowing three remote days per week, while others insist on only one. Employees begin comparing policies across teams, leading to feelings of unfairness and resentment.

This represents organizational conflict—tensions that arise from systemic issues, policy changes, or structural decisions. These conflicts often feel particularly challenging because they stem from factors beyond any individual's immediate control.

As a supervisor, you may find yourself caught in the middle of organizational conflicts, having to implement policies you didn't create while managing your team's reactions to them. Your role in these situations is crucial—you must balance being a representative of the organization with being an advocate for your team.

The Cultural Dimension

In today's global workplace, each type of conflict can be complicated by cultural differences. What might be seen as healthy direct communication in one culture could be perceived as confrontational in another. A deadline that seems flexible in one cultural context might be viewed as absolute in another.

Consider the case of a multinational team working on a project. An American team member might voice disagreement openly in meetings, viewing it as constructive feedback. However, their Japanese colleague might find this direct approach uncomfortable, preferring to raise concerns more subtly or in private conversations.

Understanding these cultural nuances isn't just about avoiding conflict—it's about leveraging diverse perspectives to create stronger solutions. As a supervisor, your awareness of cultural differences can transform potential points of tension into opportunities for learning and growth.

The Role of Power and Position

Each type of conflict is further influenced by power dynamics within the organization. A disagreement between peers takes on different dimensions when it involves a supervisor and their direct report. The same conflict that might be openly debated between colleagues often goes unspoken when power differences come into play.

As a supervisor, you must be particularly sensitive to these power dynamics. Your position gives you authority, but it also creates barriers. Employees may be hesitant to express disagreement with you directly, leading to unresolved tensions that manifest in other ways.

The Foundation: EI in Conflict Resolution

Picture yourself in this situation: Two of your best employees are in a heated argument. Your instinct is to jump in and solve the problem immediately. But something makes you pause. You notice your own tension, take a deep breath, and realize that rushing in might only escalate the situation. This moment of self-awareness—this ability to recognize and manage your own emotions while reading those of others—is EI in action.

For supervisors navigating workplace conflict, EI isn't just a helpful skill—it's the foundation upon which all effective conflict resolution is built. Think of it as your internal GPS system, helping you navigate the complex terrain of human emotions and relationships.

The Four Pillars of EI

Sarah had been a supervisor for just 3 months when she faced her first major team conflict. Two senior team members were barely speaking to each other, causing project delays and team tension. Sarah's first impulse was to call them both into her office and demand they work it out. Instead, she paused to consider her approach.

First, she examined her own feelings about the situation (self-awareness). She recognized her anxiety about handling her first major conflict and her frustration with the team's decreased productivity. Rather than let these emotions drive her actions, she consciously chose to approach the situation with curiosity instead of judgment (self-regulation).

Before speaking with either employee, Sarah spent time understanding each person's perspective (empathy). She learned that one team member was dealing with personal challenges at home, while the other felt their expertise wasn't being respected. Armed with these insights, Sarah used her relationship-building skills (social awareness) to bring the two together for a productive conversation.

This scenario illustrates the four key components of EI that every supervisor must master to handle conflict effectively.

Self-Awareness: Your Internal Compass

Think of self-awareness as your emotional radar system. It's your ability to recognize your own triggers, biases, and emotional responses to conflict. When a team member challenges your decision in a meeting, do you feel your defenses rising? When you need to deliver difficult feedback, does anxiety make you want to postpone the conversation?

These reactions are natural, but left unexamined, they can hijack your ability to handle conflict effectively. The self-aware supervisor recognizes these emotional responses without being controlled by them.

Consider this: You're about to have a difficult conversation with an underperforming employee. Before the meeting, you notice tension in your shoulders and a knot in your stomach. Instead of ignoring these physical signs of stress, you acknowledge them. This awareness allows you to take a few deep breaths, review your talking points, and enter the conversation in a more centered state.

Self-Regulation: The Art of Emotional Balance

If self-awareness is about recognizing your emotions, self-regulation is about managing them effectively. It's your ability to stay calm and clear-headed, even when emotions run high around you.

Imagine you're mediating a heated dispute between two team members. One makes a personal attack against the other. Your immediate impulse might be to shut down the conversation out of discomfort. Instead, self-regulation allows you to remain composed, redirect the conversation productively, and model the emotional control you want to see from your team.

Self-regulation doesn't mean suppressing emotions—it means choosing how to express them appropriately. When an employee raises their voice in frustration, the self-regulated supervisor doesn't match their intensity. Instead, they might say, "I can see this is really important to you. Let's take a moment to discuss this calmly so I can better understand your concerns."

Empathy: The Bridge Builder

Empathy is your ability to understand and acknowledge others' emotions and perspectives, even when they differ from your own. It's not about agreeing with everyone—it's about recognizing that their feelings and viewpoints are valid to them.

A supervisor was mediating a conflict between two team members about project responsibilities. Instead of immediately jumping to solutions, she first acknowledged each person's frustration: "John, I hear that you feel overwhelmed with your current workload. Maria, I understand you're concerned about meeting the client's expectations. Let's figure out how we can address both of these valid concerns."

This approach doesn't solve the problem immediately, but it creates the psychological safety necessary for productive problem solving. When people feel heard and understood, they're more likely to engage in finding solutions rather than defending their positions.

Social Skills: The Master Conductor

The final component of EI involves using your understanding of emotions to build and maintain relationships. Think of it as the practical application of the other three components—how you use your self-awareness, self-regulation, and empathy to navigate social situations effectively.

For supervisors, strong social skills mean knowing how to:

- Choose the right time and place for difficult conversations
- Frame feedback in a way that maintains dignity and respect
- Build coalitions to support conflict resolution
- Repair relationships after conflicts have been resolved

A skilled supervisor noticed growing tension between her sales and marketing teams. Instead of calling a group meeting to address the issue, she first had informal conversations with key team members. She learned about each department's challenges and perspectives. When she finally brought everyone together, she could facilitate the conversation in a way that acknowledged each team's concerns while focusing on shared goals.

The Power of Practice

Like any skill, EI grows stronger with conscious practice. Each difficult conversation becomes an opportunity to:

- Notice your emotional reactions (self-awareness)
- Choose your responses thoughtfully (self-regulation)
- Understand others' perspectives (empathy)
- Build stronger relationships (social skills)

Remember: The goal isn't to become immune to emotions in the workplace. Rather, it's to develop the EI to navigate them effectively, turning potential conflicts into opportunities for growth and understanding.

The Art of Conflict Resolution: A Step-by-Step Approach

Understanding conflict types and developing EI creates the foundation for effective conflict resolution. But when you're faced with an actual conflict situation, how do you put this knowledge into practice? Let's explore a systematic approach that turns theory into action.

The First Five Minutes: Setting the Stage

James, a new supervisor in a technology company, received an urgent message from his team lead: two key developers weren't speaking to each other, putting an important project at risk. His instinct was to call an immediate meeting and demand they work together. Instead, he remembered a crucial principle: the first five minutes of addressing any conflict often determine its ultimate resolution.

Before taking action, James asked himself three critical questions:

- What do I know about the situation?
- What don't I know?
- What's the potential impact if I handle this poorly?

This brief moment of reflection prevented him from rushing into a situation that required careful handling. It's a practice that every supervisor should cultivate—the pause before action that can make the difference between resolving a conflict and escalating it.

Step 1: Gather Intelligence

Think of yourself as a detective in the early stages of conflict resolution. Your goal isn't to make immediate judgments but to understand the full picture. This means gathering information from multiple sources while maintaining appropriate confidentiality.

When Elena noticed increasing tension between her sales and customer service teams, she didn't immediately call a group meeting. Instead, she:

- Had informal conversations with team members from both departments
- Reviewed recent incident reports and customer feedback
- Observed team interactions during regular meetings
- Noted patterns in when and how conflicts typically arose

This investigation revealed that the root cause wasn't personality conflicts, as she'd initially assumed, but rather misaligned incentive structures that put the departments at odds with each other.

The lesson? Surface-level conflicts often mask deeper systemic issues. Taking time to understand the full context helps you address root causes rather than just symptoms.

Step 2: Create a Safe Space for Dialogue

With a clearer understanding of the situation, your next step is to create an environment where honest, productive conversations can take place. This involves both physical and psychological safety.

Consider Maria's approach when handling a conflict between two long-term employees. She:

- Chose a neutral meeting space, not her office
- Scheduled the conversation when both parties were fresh, not at the end of a long day
- Established clear ground rules for the discussion
- Started by acknowledging both employees' contributions to the team

Most importantly, she began the conversation with a statement that set the tone: "We're here to understand each other better and find a way forward that works for everyone. This isn't about finding fault—it's about finding solutions."

Step 3: Active Listening and Validation

Once you've created a safe space, the real work begins. Active listening isn't just about hearing words—it's about understanding meanings, emotions, and underlying needs.

A supervisor named David demonstrated this skill masterfully during a team conflict. When each person spoke, he:

- Maintained eye contact
- Took notes on key points
- Reflected back what he heard: "Let me make sure I understand..."
- Acknowledged emotions: "I can hear how frustrating this has been..."
- Asked clarifying questions: "Can you tell me more about that?"

Most importantly, he resisted the urge to jump in with solutions. This patience allowed team members to feel truly heard and often led them to discover solutions on their own.

Step 4: Guide the Conversation Toward Solutions

With understanding established, the next step is moving from problems to solutions. This transition requires skill—push too quickly, and people may feel their concerns aren't fully heard; move too slowly, and the conversation can get stuck in complaint mode.

Sarah, a production supervisor, used a simple but effective technique to make this transition. After ensuring everyone had shared their perspectives, she asked: "Now that we understand the challenges better, what do you think could help improve this situation?"

This question accomplished several things:

- It acknowledged that the previous discussion was valuable.
- It shifted focus from past problems to future solutions.
- It invited participation rather than imposing answers.
- It emphasized shared responsibility for finding solutions.

Step 5: Create Clear Agreements

The final step in conflict resolution is perhaps the most crucial: turning dialogue into action. Without clear agreements, even the most productive conversations can fail to create lasting change.

When Alex mediated a conflict between two departments, he ended the meeting by having everyone agree on:

- Specific actions to be taken
- Who would take each action
- Timeline for completion
- How progress would be measured
- When they would follow up to review progress

He documented these agreements in a brief e-mail to all participants, making sure everyone had the same understanding of next steps.

The Follow-Through: Making Changes Stick

Resolution isn't a one-time event—it's a process that requires follow-up and reinforcement. Successful supervisors schedule regular check-ins to:

- Monitor progress on agreements
- Address any new concerns quickly
- Acknowledge and celebrate improvements
- Adjust approaches if needed

This ongoing attention sends a powerful message: resolving conflict isn't just about putting out fires—it's about building stronger, more resilient teams.

Mastering Difficult Conversations: Common Scenarios

While the principles of conflict resolution remain constant, different types of difficult conversations require unique approaches. Let's explore some of the most challenging situations supervisors face and strategies for handling them effectively.

The Performance Conversation

Mark had been avoiding this conversation for weeks. An otherwise strong employee's performance had been slipping for months. Projects were late, quality was inconsistent, and team members were starting to complain. Mark knew he needed to address the situation, but he worried about damaging what had been a positive working relationship.

This scenario is familiar to most supervisors. Performance conversations are often the most dreaded type of difficult discussion. Yet when handled skillfully, they can strengthen relationships and improve outcomes.

Consider how an experienced supervisor named Lisa handled a similar situation:

First, she prepared thoroughly:

- Gathered specific examples of performance issues
- Documented the impact on the team and organization

- Reviewed the employee's past performance records
- Prepared potential solutions and support options

Then, she structured the conversation carefully:

Tom, I've noticed some changes in your work over the past few months that I'd like to discuss. Recently, the Johnson project was delivered two weeks late, and the client report needed significant revisions. This isn't typical of your usual high standards, and I'm concerned. I'd like to understand what's happening and see how I can support you.

Notice how Lisa:

- Started with observation, not judgment
- Used specific examples
- Acknowledged past good performance
- Showed genuine concern
- Offered support

The conversation revealed that Tom was struggling with new project management software and felt embarrassed to ask for help. Together, they developed a plan that included additional training and regular check-ins.

Navigating Team Conflicts

Sarah walked into what she thought would be a routine team meeting to find two of her senior developers in a heated argument about coding standards. The tension had clearly been building for weeks, and now it was affecting the entire team's dynamics.

Team conflicts present unique challenges because they often involve multiple perspectives and complex group dynamics. However, they also offer opportunities for strengthening team cohesion when handled well.

A supervisor named Michael successfully navigated a similar situation using this approach:

First, he addressed the immediate tension: "I can see there are strong feelings about our coding standards. Let's pause for a moment and make sure we can discuss this productively."

Then, he reframed the conflict as a shared challenge: "We all want our code to be both efficient and maintainable. Let's understand each perspective and find a solution that works for the whole team."

Finally, he facilitated a structured discussion where:

- Each person shared their perspective without interruption.
- The team identified shared goals and concerns.
- They collaborated on guidelines that incorporated both viewpoints.
- They established a process for handling future disagreements.

The Remote Element: Handling Virtual Conflicts

The rise of remote and hybrid work has added new complexities to conflict resolution. When Jennifer noticed increasing tension between team members across different time zones, she realized that virtual conflicts required special consideration.

Virtual conflicts can escalate quickly because:

- Nonverbal cues are often missed.
- Messages can be misinterpreted.
- Time zones can delay resolution.
- Cultural nuances are harder to navigate.

Jennifer developed specific strategies for virtual conflict resolution:
For one-on-one conflicts:

- Used video calls whenever possible
- Scheduled conversations when both parties were fresh
- Sent brief follow-up e-mails documenting agreements
- Checked in more frequently during implementation

For team conflicts:

- Created structured virtual meetings with clear agendas
- Used collaborative tools to ensure all voices were heard
- Established communication protocols for different situations
- Built in regular team-building activities

The Organizational Change Conversation

When David's company announced a major restructuring, he found himself having to explain difficult changes to his team. Some roles would be eliminated, others would change significantly, and everyone was anxious about the future.

These conversations are particularly challenging because:

- The supervisor often doesn't have all the answers
- Changes may affect people's livelihoods
- Emotions run high
- Trust is essential but fragile

David approached these conversations with a framework he called "Truth, Empathy, and Path Forward":

Truth: He shared what he knew clearly and directly: "I want to be upfront about the changes coming to our department. Here's what I know for certain, what's still being decided, and what timeline we're working with."

Empathy: He acknowledged the impact: "I understand this creates uncertainty and anxiety. Your concerns are valid, and I want to hear them."

Path Forward: He focused on next steps: "While some things are outside our control, let's discuss what we can do to prepare for these changes and support each other through this transition."

Cross-Cultural Considerations

When Ming joined as a supervisor in a multinational company, she quickly learned that conflict resolution styles varied significantly across cultures. What worked in one context could be counterproductive in another.

Consider these variations:

- Some cultures value direct communication, while others prefer indirect approaches.
- The role of hierarchy and authority differs across cultures.
- The importance of "saving face" varies significantly.
- Attitudes toward conflict itself range from viewing it as necessary to seeing it as deeply problematic.

Ming developed an approach that she called "Cultural Bridge Building": First, she educated herself:

- Learned about different cultural approaches to conflict
- Asked team members about their preferences
- Observed successful conflict resolution in different cultural contexts

Then, she adapted her style:

- Used a mix of direct and indirect communication
- Offered multiple channels for raising concerns
- Respected cultural preferences while maintaining fairness
- Created clear frameworks that could flex to different cultural needs

Knowing When to Seek Help

Even the most skilled supervisors sometimes encounter situations that require additional support. Recognizing when to seek help isn't a sign of failure—it's a mark of wisdom and professional judgment.

When Rachel noticed that a conflict between two team members involved allegations of harassment, she knew she needed to involve HR immediately. "As supervisors, we need to know not just how to handle conflicts, but also when to bring in additional resources," she explains. "Some situations have legal or policy implications that require expertise beyond our role."

Understanding Your Resources

Think of conflict resolution resources as a toolkit. Different situations require different tools, and knowing which to use can make the difference between resolution and escalation.

Human Resources: Consider HR your partner in handling complex employee relations issues. They bring expertise in:

- Policy interpretation and application
- Legal compliance
- Investigation procedures
- Documentation requirements

John, a manufacturing supervisor, learned this lesson when handling a complex performance issue. "I thought I could manage it on my own," he recalls. "But when I consulted HR, they helped me see potential complications I hadn't considered and guided me through the proper procedures."

Employee assistance programs (EAP)—Many organizations offer EAP services—confidential resources for employees dealing with personal or professional challenges. These programs can be invaluable when conflicts have underlying personal dimensions.

Professional mediators—Some situations benefit from external, neutral facilitation. Professional mediators bring:

- Objectivity
- Specialized conflict resolution skills
- Fresh perspectives
- No organizational history or bias

When to Escalate

Certain situations require immediate escalation:

Legal or ethical issues: When Sara discovered that a conflict between team members involved potential discrimination, she immediately contacted HR. "In these situations, proper handling isn't just important—it's legally required," she explains.

Safety concerns: Any conflict involving threats, harassment, or safety concerns requires immediate escalation to appropriate authorities, including HR, security, or law enforcement, when necessary.

Pattern issues: Sometimes conflicts indicate broader organizational issues. Maria noticed that similar conflicts kept arising around the same processes. "That's when I realized we needed to involve senior leadership to address systemic problems," she shares.

Preventing Future Conflicts

While some conflict is inevitable, many conflicts can be prevented through intentional leadership practices. Let's explore how successful supervisors create environments that minimize destructive conflict while encouraging productive disagreement.

Building Strong Foundations

Alex inherited a team known for its conflict issues. Rather than addressing each dispute as it arose, he focused on strengthening the team's foundation:

Clear expectations—Alex worked with the team to establish:

- Documented processes for common situations
- Decision-making frameworks
- Communication protocols
- Role clarity

Regular Communication—Alex implemented:

- Weekly one-on-ones with team members
- Monthly team meetings focused on process improvement
- Open-door hours for informal discussions
- Regular feedback sessions

Team development—Alex invested in:

- Team-building activities
- Cross-training opportunities

- Conflict resolution training
- Cultural awareness workshops

The Impact of Preventive Measures

Over time, Alex's team transformed. "We still have disagreements," he notes, "but now they're primarily about ideas and improvements rather than interpersonal issues. The team has learned to disagree productively."

Early Warning Systems

Lisa developed what she calls her "conflict radar"—the ability to spot potential issues before they escalate. She watches for:

Changes in behavior

- Unusual silence from typically engaged team members
- Increased tension in meetings
- Changes in communication patterns
- Decreased collaboration

Team dynamic shifts

- Formation of cliques
- Changes in social interactions
- Increased complaints about small issues
- Decreased volunteering for shared tasks

When she notices these signs, she takes proactive steps:

- Informal check-ins with team members
- Team pulse surveys
- Process reviews
- Preemptive discussions about potential issues

Conclusion: Your Journey as a Conflict-Capable Leader

Becoming skilled at handling conflict is not about eliminating disagreements altogether—it's about learning to navigate them with confidence, clarity, and purpose. Conflict, when managed effectively, becomes an opportunity for growth, stronger relationships, and improved team dynamics. As you continue developing your leadership skills, remember that every difficult conversation is a steppingstone toward becoming a more capable and resilient leader.

One way to track your progress is by keeping a conflict resolution journal. Use it to document workplace disputes, note what strategies worked or fell short, and reflect on key lessons learned. Over time, this practice will help you refine your approach, identify patterns, and develop a deeper understanding of your own conflict management style.

Here are five key principles to keep in mind as you apply what you've learned:

1. **Conflict itself isn't the problem—it's how we handle it that matters.** Avoiding conflict rarely makes it disappear; addressing it constructively leads to resolution and growth.
2. **Preparation and prevention are just as important as resolution.** Proactive communication, clear expectations, and early intervention can prevent many conflicts before they escalate.
3. **Your role is to guide, not to fix.** A supervisor's job is not to impose solutions but to facilitate conversations that empower employees to resolve their own disputes.
4. **Sometimes, seeking help is the best course of action.** Knowing when to involve HR, senior leadership, or mediation services is a sign of wisdom, not weakness.
5. **Every conflict presents an opportunity to strengthen relationships and improve processes.** Handled well, conflicts can lead to more trust, collaboration, and team alignment.

The mark of an effective supervisor is not the absence of conflict, but the ability to **navigate it skillfully, address it fairly, and turn challenges into opportunities.** With the frameworks and tools from this chapter, you are well-prepared to handle difficult conversations with professionalism and confidence.

Your next difficult conversation isn't just a challenge to overcome—it's an opportunity to **demonstrate leadership, build trust, and foster a healthier team culture.** Approach it with the mindset of growth, knowing that conflict, when handled well, is a steppingstone to stronger leadership.

Just a reminder, be sure to complete the worksheets before moving on to the next chapter.

CHAPTER 7

Supporting Team Development and Growth

Helping your team grow is like planting a garden—nurture their potential, give them space, and watch them flourish.

A supervisor's role extends beyond overseeing daily tasks; it involves fostering an environment where individuals grow, collaborate, and contribute to long-term organizational success. When supervisors focus on team development, they're not just investing in individuals—they're cultivating the collective capability of their teams. Research from MIT's Human Dynamics Laboratory highlights that high-performing teams are shaped significantly by their communication patterns, with face-to-face exchanges accounting for 35 percent of performance variation and social interactions contributing to more than 50 percent of positive changes in communication behaviors (Pentland 2012). These insights underscore an essential reality for new supervisors: Developing a successful team requires more than just assigning tasks and tracking outcomes—it requires a commitment to continuous learning, mentorship, and professional development.

The Strategic Imperative of Development

The business case for structured team development is compelling. Gallup's research indicates that highly engaged teams experience 21 percent higher profitability and 17 percent higher productivity compared with their less engaged counterparts (Gallup 2020). Similarly, organizations with strong learning cultures are 37 percent more productive, 32 percent more likely to be first to market, and 17 percent more likely to be market leaders in their segment (Bersin & Associates 2010). LinkedIn's 2019 Workforce Learning Report revealed that 94 percent of employees would stay at a company longer if it invested in their learning and development (LinkedIn 2019). A prime example is Microsoft, which implemented a growth mindset development framework that contributed to its market cap tripling between 2014 and 2019. These statistics underscore a crucial fact: Investing in development not only benefits employees but drives measurable business success.

Beyond the Annual Review: A New Paradigm

Traditional approaches to team development, such as annual performance reviews, are increasingly seen as insufficient in today's fast-paced work environment. According to a study by Deloitte, companies that have adopted continuous performance management models report improved employee engagement (with 90 percent direct improvements), greater process simplicity, and higher-quality conversations between managers and employees (Deloite 2017), Similarly, McKinsey research emphasizes that organizations fostering a culture of continuous learning and feedback show significantly higher rates of employee retention and are better positioned to lead innovation in their industries (McKinsey 2021).

For new supervisors, this shift means moving beyond static evaluations and embracing an ongoing coaching mindset. Successful supervisors actively facilitate growth by:

- Helping employees identify and leverage their strengths
- Providing guidance on career development opportunities
- Encouraging skill building and cross-functional learning
- Connecting individual growth with broader organizational goals

Supervisors who adopt this proactive approach not only elevate individual performance but also create an agile, future-ready workforce equipped for long-term success.

The Development Imperative

Supporting team development is more than just skill building—it's about fostering a workplace culture where growth is expected, supported, and celebrated. According to LinkeIn's Workplace Learning Report (2019), 94 percent of employees said they would stay at a company longer if their organization invested in their learning and development. Similarly, Gallup's research shows that highly engaged teams—often the result of strong development support—experience 23 percent higher profitability and 18 percent high productivity (Gallup 2022).

This means that the most effective supervisors don't just provide training opportunities; they create environments where employees are encouraged to take ownership of their professional growth, seek new challenges, and contribute meaningfully to the team's success.

Building Team Excellence: A Practical Guide to Development

This chapter explores proven strategies for fostering team growth and development. Drawing from Gallup and LinkeIn Learning, we will examine approaches that deliver measurable results in performance, engagement, and retention. From crafting personalized development plans to leveraging mentorship and feedback loops, the goal is to equip you with actionable techniques that elevate both individual and team success.

Remember, effective team development isn't about grand initiatives—it's about the consistent, intentional actions that build capability over time. Let's begin by exploring how to create development plans that drive real results.

As you move through this chapter, think about your role as a *gardener of potential*. Some employees may need a little extra sun (encouragement), others may require pruning (constructive feedback), and still others may need deeper roots (foundational skills) before they can grow tall. Your job is to cultivate the conditions that allow growth to happen naturally, while also stepping in with support when necessary.

Growth is a process, not an event. By the end of this chapter, you'll have the tools, mindset, and strategies to support your team's development in meaningful and lasting ways. The seeds you plant today will yield a stronger, more capable team tomorrow.

Development Plans and Growth Opportunities

Introduction: The Launchpad for Success

Supporting the development and growth of your team is one of the most impactful responsibilities of a supervisor. It's not just about ensuring employees meet their current performance targets; it's about unlocking their potential for future roles and responsibilities. Supervisors who master this skill become transformational leaders, building stronger, more capable teams and increasing engagement, retention, and organizational success.

Growth and development don't happen by chance. They require a clear plan, intentional effort, and an environment that supports learning. Supervisors play a pivotal role as facilitators, coaches, and mentors, helping employees set career goals, acquire new skills, and step outside their comfort zones. When done effectively, development and growth initiatives result in highly engaged employees, cohesive teams, and organizations that are ready for the future.

This section will provide first-time supervisors—and those looking to refine their skills—with the knowledge, tools, and strategies to build a culture of development and growth within their teams. From Individualized Development Plans (IDPs) to mentorship and growth mindset principles, this chapter will give you a complete guide to becoming a growth-oriented supervisor.

The Power of Personalized Development Plans: The Blueprint for Success

One of the most powerful tools at your disposal is the DP. It provides a clear, actionable roadmap for growth, offering structure to the often nebulous concept of "development." IDPs align individual ambitions with organizational goals, ensuring employees aren't just growing for growth's sake—they're growing with purpose.

A successful IDP includes collaborative goal setting, clear milestones, and regular check-ins. As a supervisor, your role is to facilitate open, honest conversations about career goals, skills gaps, and opportunities for growth. These conversations build trust and demonstrate your genuine interest in the employee's future.

But IDPs aren't just about setting goals—they're about achieving them. By breaking large goals into smaller, actionable steps with measurable milestones, employees can see progress in real time. This process motivates employees to stay on track and fosters a sense of accomplishment along the way.

Key Takeaways for Supervisors:

- Make it collaborative: Build the plan *with* your employees, not *for* them.
- Focus on the whole employee: Include short-term skill development and long-term career aspirations.
- Track progress and adapt: Revisit the plan regularly to ensure it's still relevant and achievable.

When employees have clarity on their future and know that their supervisor is actively invested in their success, they feel empowered, engaged, and committed to doing their best work.

Components of an Effective IDP

a. **Collaborative Process**

Growth is most effective when supervisors and employees work together to create the IDP. Here's how to make this process collaborative and meaningful:

- Start with a conversation: Schedule 1:1 discussions to understand the employee's interests, motivations, and aspirations.
- Skills gap analysis: Assess the employee's current skills and identify areas for growth.
- Create alignment: Link individual goals to team or organizational priorities.
- Set check-in milestones: Establish quarterly or monthly check-ins to review progress and make adjustments.

b. **Short- and Long-Term Goals**

Effective IDPs balance short-term goals (3–6 months) with long-term goals (1–5 years). Goals should follow the SMART framework—Specific, Measurable, Achievable, Relevant, and Time-bound.

- ○ **Short-term goals**: These focus on immediate skills, knowledge, or project-based achievements. Examples include mastering new software, attending a workshop, or completing a certification.
- ○ **Long-term goals**: These focus on broader career aspirations, like becoming a team lead, taking on more strategic projects, or preparing for a promotion.

c. **Measurable Milestones**

Milestones help supervisors and employees measure progress. Without them, growth remains abstract.

- ○ **Break down big goals**: Divide long-term objectives into smaller tasks with clear deadlines.
- ○ **Use visual tracking tools**: Tools like Trello or Google Sheets can help employees visualize their progress.
- ○ **Celebrate wins**: Recognize small achievements to maintain motivation.

Example in Action

Sarah at InnovateTech collaborated with her team to create IDPs. One employee, a software developer, wanted to learn Python, while another sought leadership training. They set short-term goals (complete an online course) and long-term goals (apply for leadership training) and reviewed progress during monthly check-ins. As a result, both employees demonstrated enhanced skills and greater motivation.

Benefits of IDPs

- Increased engagement: Employees feel seen, heard, and valued.
- Clarity and direction: Employees understand their next steps for growth.
- Retention: Employees who see a future for themselves within the organization are more likely to stay.

Challenges of IDPs

- Time commitment: Creating and maintaining IDPs requires regular conversations and follow-ups.

- Employee buy-in: Not all employees will immediately see the value of an IDP. Supervisors must communicate its importance.

Identifying Growth Opportunities on the Job: The Engine of Development

If IDPs are the blueprint, then growth opportunities are the engine that drives development forward. Without opportunities to apply new skills, development becomes theoretical and stagnant. Growth happens when employees are challenged, stretched, and exposed to new experiences.

As a supervisor, your role is to create a continuous cycle of challenge, support, and feedback. Growth opportunities come in many forms, from stretch assignments and job rotations to mentorships and temporary leadership roles. They allow employees to move out of their comfort zone and build confidence in their abilities.

Growth opportunities don't have to be complicated. You don't always need to send employees to week-long training programs or expensive workshops. Sometimes, the most impactful opportunities exist within the work you're already doing. For example, invite employees to lead a meeting, manage a small project, or serve as a mentor to a newer teammate. These "micro-opportunities" add up over time and prepare employees for larger roles in the future.

Key Takeaways for Supervisors:

- Prioritize stretch assignments: Stretch assignments build confidence and capability.
- Provide real-world challenges: Growth happens faster when employees face real problems, not theoretical exercises.
- Incorporate on-the-job learning: Learning happens naturally when employees are given new tasks and challenges.

Supervisors who embed growth into daily work create teams that are constantly learning, improving, and innovating. Every project, task, and interaction becomes a development opportunity.

Key Steps for Work Alignment

a. **Identify Organizational Priorities**
   - Review the company's strategic plan, upcoming projects, and anticipated skills gaps.
   - Connect development goals to company needs (e.g., upskilling team members in AI if the company is moving toward automation).

b. **Encourage Role-Specific Skills Development**

   - Identify competencies critical to the success of specific roles and focus development efforts there.

Example in Action

IBM famously reduced turnover in the 1950s and 1960s by tailoring IDPs to align with its goals. Employees developed technical skills relevant to IBM's strategic priorities, fostering a highly skilled, loyal workforce.

Benefits of Alignment

- Cohesive teams: Everyone is moving toward the same goals.
- Organizational agility: Teams are prepared for changes in strategy, technology, and industry shifts.

Challenges of Alignment

- Resistance to change: Employees may resist development initiatives they don't immediately see as relevant.
- Supervisor burden: It requires time and effort to align individual development goals with organizational objectives.

Building a Culture of Learning and Curiosity

Supporting team development goes beyond ensuring employees meet the minimum requirements of their roles. It's about unlocking potential, fostering continuous growth, and guiding team members to achieve their fullest capabilities. Great supervisors recognize that every employee represents untapped potential waiting to be discovered. By investing in development, supervisors don't just create better employees—they create stronger teams, more resilient organizations, and, ultimately, better leaders of their own.

Development isn't a "nice-to-have"—it's essential for long-term success. When supervisors prioritize growth, they build teams that are engaged, agile, and ready to meet future challenges. Employees who feel seen, valued, and supported in their career aspirations are more loyal, more productive, and more willing to go the extra mile. As a supervisor, you have the power to create a work environment where growth is not only encouraged but expected.

But how does a supervisor achieve this? It starts with intention and commitment. By creating IDPs, offering diverse growth opportunities, and fostering a culture of continuous learning, you lay the foundation for a team that doesn't just meet expectations—it exceeds them.

IDPs and growth opportunities are critical, but without a culture of continuous learning, development can stall. A learning culture promotes curiosity, experimentation, and exploration. It encourages employees to ask questions, seek out new knowledge, and try new approaches without fear of failure.

Continuous learning isn't about perfection; it's about progress. Supervisors who foster this culture recognize that mistakes are part of the learning process. Instead of punishing errors, they turn them into teachable moments. This shift from "failure as punishment" to "failure as growth" creates a psychologically safe environment where people feel comfortable taking risks.

Creating a learning culture requires supervisors to model the behaviors they want to see. If you want employees to embrace learning, you must be willing to learn alongside them. Participate in training sessions, admit your mistakes, and share the lessons you've learned from your own failures. When supervisors model a growth mindset, employees follow.

Key Takeaways for Supervisors:

- Embrace a growth mindset: Treat mistakes as learning opportunities, not failures.

- Encourage lifelong learning: Provide access to courses, workshops, and self-study programs.
- Recognize learning milestones: Acknowledge when employees take risks, experiment, and learn something new.

A team that learns together grows together. By fostering a continuous learning environment, you ensure your team is ready for whatever challenges come next.

Types of Growth Opportunities

Training and Education

- Provide access to workshops, certifications, and e-learning platforms.

Stretch Assignments

- Assign employees to projects outside their comfort zone.
- Example: Alex at TechNova paired junior developers with senior developers on a project, which boosted collaboration and accelerated learning.

Mentorship

- Internal mentorship: Employees are paired with senior colleagues for guidance.
- Peer mentorship: Colleagues support each other's growth and knowledge-sharing.

Growth Mindset Initiatives

- Promote learning as a continual process, not a one-time event.
- Create safe spaces for failure, turning mistakes into teachable moments.

Example in Action

Sarah at InnovateTech implemented "Failure Fridays," where team members shared mistakes they made and what they learned. It built psychological safety and reduced fear of failure.

Benefits of Growth Opportunities

- Skill development: Teams become more agile, adaptable, and future-ready.
- Motivation: Employees stay engaged when they feel challenged.

Challenges of Growth Opportunities

- Resistance to stretch assignments: Employees may feel nervous about tasks that push them out of their comfort zone.
- Resource constraints: Offering formal learning opportunities requires time and money.

The Supervisor as a Coach, Mentor, and Champion of Professional Growth

Development and growth require a different type of supervisor. It's no longer enough to be a "manager" who focuses on tasks and deadlines. Today's most effective leaders are coaches, mentors, and champions of growth.

As a coach, your role is to ask questions, not provide answers. Coaches encourage self-reflection, guide employees to solve their own problems, and offer support along the way. This builds confidence and self-sufficiency.

As a mentor, you offer your own experiences, insights, and wisdom. You help employees see the bigger picture and identify growth paths they may not have considered.

As a champion of growth, you advocate for your team's development at higher levels of the organization. Whether it's requesting a training budget, nominating employees for leadership programs, or assigning employees to high-visibility projects, you play an active role in positioning your team members for success.

Key Takeaways for Supervisors

- Ask, don't tell: Use coaching questions like "What would you do differently next time?"
- Be available for guidance: Employees need access to their supervisor for career advice and development support.
- Be their advocate: Nominate employees for training, certification, and leadership programs.

When employees see their supervisor as someone who genuinely cares about their growth, they're more engaged, loyal, and eager to contribute.

How to Become a Growth-Oriented Coach

Supervisors aren't just task managers; they're coaches. Here's how supervisors can become growth-oriented coaches:

- Set career goals: Help employees clarify where they want to go and how they'll get there.
- Offer feedback and guidance: Provide timely, specific, and constructive feedback.
- Foster a growth mindset: Encourage employees to see setbacks as opportunities for growth.

Example in Action

Alex at TechNova coached employees after a project presentation. He praised their strengths and framed areas for improvement as growth opportunities, which resulted in a more confident team.

Outcome

When supervisors take on the role of coach, mentor, and champion of growth, employees experience heightened engagement, increased confidence, and accelerated development. Teams become more self-sufficient, resilient, and innovative. By fostering a culture of growth, supervisors build stronger, more adaptable teams that are prepared to meet future challenges. Organizations benefit from higher employee retention, improved performance, and a robust internal talent pipeline. Ultimately, the supervisor's success is reflected in the growth and achievements of their team members.

Leveraging Feedback for Development

Building on the feedback principles explored in previous chapters, supervisors can use structured feedback to accelerate team development and professional growth. Feedback, when delivered effectively, serves as both a performance enhancer and a learning catalyst. Research from Deloitte (2024) shows that teams implementing structured developmental feedback experience:

- 45 percent faster skill acquisition
- 37 percent higher engagement in learning initiatives
- 52 percent better career progression rates

Effective developmental feedback goes beyond evaluating past performance—it provides a roadmap for continuous improvement. Supervisors should create an environment where feedback is frequent, specific, and action-oriented. This means offering both positive reinforcement to strengthen successful behaviors and constructive feedback to guide improvements.

For example, instead of saying, *"You need to improve your client presentations,"* a more effective approach would be: *"During your last client presentation, you provided strong data analysis but could increase engagement by using real-world examples. Let's set up a time to review techniques for audience interaction.*" This type of feedback not only clarifies expectations but also empowers employees with a clear development path.

Supervisors should also encourage peer feedback, fostering a culture where team members support each other's growth. When feedback becomes an ongoing dialogue rather than an annual event, employees are more likely to embrace learning, refine their skills, and take ownership of their career development.

Transforming Feedback into Development Opportunities

While previous discussions have focused on the mechanics of feedback delivery, it is equally important to understand how feedback can be used as a tool for continuous development. Effective feedback does not just assess past performance—it guides future growth. To achieve this, supervisors should focus on three key strategies:

1. **Growth-Focused Conversations**
   Instead of merely addressing past actions, developmental feedback should encourage employees to think about how they can grow and improve in the future. This means shifting the conversation from *what happened* to *what's possible.* Thought-provoking questions can help employees connect feedback to their long-term development:
   - "How might this experience help you in future leadership roles?"
   - "What skills could you develop to handle similar situations even better?"
   - "What resources or support would help you build on this success?"

   By framing feedback as an opportunity for learning, supervisors empower employees to take an active role in their professional development.

2. **Learning-Centered Follow-Up**
   Feedback should not be a one-time conversation—it should lead to concrete actions that facilitate learning and skill development. Supervisors can help employees translate feedback into actionable steps by:
   - Identifying relevant training or upskilling opportunities.

- Connecting employees with mentors or experienced colleagues.
- Assigning stretch projects that build on their strengths.
- Creating practice opportunities for newly acquired skills.

   By ensuring feedback discussions lead to specific developmental actions, supervisors reinforce a culture of continuous learning and improvement.

3. **Building Development Momentum**

   To make feedback an ongoing driver of growth, supervisors should establish regular touchpoints to track progress and maintain motivation. This includes:

   - Setting periodic check-ins to review development goals and refine approaches
   - Adjusting learning strategies based on employee progress and challenges
   - Recognizing and celebrating small growth milestones to reinforce motivation
   - Connecting individual achievements to broader team and organizational success

   This structured approach ensures that feedback serves as a catalyst for continuous development rather than merely a performance evaluation tool. By integrating feedback into regular development discussions, supervisors create a work environment where improvement is not just encouraged—it is expected and supported.

Overcoming Development Roadblocks

Every employee's path to growth is unique, but roadblocks are a shared experience. Development obstacles can slow progress, create frustration, and limit potential. Effective supervisors recognize these barriers and take proactive steps to address them.

Common Development Roadblocks

- **Lack of clarity:** Employees struggle when expectations and success criteria are ambiguous.

- **Fear of failure:** Hesitation to take risks limits development opportunities.
- **Limited resources:** Without adequate training, tools, or time, employees can't advance their skills.
- **Fixed mindset:** A belief that abilities are static discourages learning and growth.
- **Inadequate feedback:** Without regular, actionable feedback, employees lack direction for improvement.

How to Overcome Development Roadblocks

Supervisors play a crucial role in eliminating these barriers by:

- **Clarifying goals and expectations:** Define success clearly and break down larger objectives into manageable steps.
- **Encouraging risk-taking:** Create a safe space for learning from mistakes and recognize efforts, not just results.
- **Providing access to resources:** Ensure employees have access to training, mentorship, and development opportunities.
- **Fostering a growth mindset:** Reframe challenges as opportunities and model continuous learning.
- **Delivering consistent feedback:** Offer real-time guidance that is specific, actionable, and solution-focused.

By proactively identifying and addressing development barriers, supervisors create an environment where employees feel empowered to grow, innovate, and excel.

Example in Action

During a major product launch, Jordan's supervisor, Maya, noticed that he was hesitant to take on a leadership role. Through one-on-one coaching, Maya discovered that Jordan feared failure and wasn't sure what success looked like. She clarified the expectations, framed leadership as a growth opportunity, and shared her own experiences with overcoming self-doubt. Additionally, she set up weekly check-ins to offer feedback and support. By the end of the project, Jordan's confidence grew and he successfully led a key initiative within the launch.

Outcome

Overcoming development roadblocks leads to more engaged, confident, and capable employees. Supervisors who actively address these barriers create a culture of growth and resilience. Employees become more willing to take on new challenges, knowing they'll be supported throughout the process. This approach strengthens team performance, builds internal talent, and improves overall job satisfaction. Ultimately, organizations benefit from a more adaptable, growth-oriented workforce prepared to meet future challenges head-on.

Measuring Progress and Recognizing Achievements

Tracking progress and celebrating achievements are essential components of employee development. They provide motivation, reinforce positive behaviors, and ensure alignment with the team and organizational goals. Supervisors who actively measure progress and recognize achievements create a culture of accountability, continuous improvement, and forward momentum.

Why Measuring Progress Matters

Measuring progress isn't just about tracking numbers—it plays a fundamental role in shaping workplace behavior and engagement. Regular assessment of development efforts ensures that employees remain on track and that supervisors can provide timely support when needed. Key benefits of measuring progress include:

- **Increased accountability:** Employees are more likely to follow through on commitments when their progress is monitored.
- **Boosted motivation:** Achieving milestones fosters a sense of accomplishment and fuels continued effort.

- **Promotion of continuous improvement:** Regular tracking allows supervisors and employees to identify areas for growth and course-correct as needed.
- **Alignment of individual and team goals:** Measurement ensures that personal development efforts align with broader organizational priorities.

How to Measure Progress

Effective measurement involves clear goal setting, regular progress reviews, and constructive feedback. Supervisors can implement the following strategies:

- **Set clear, measurable goals:** Use the SMART framework (Specific, Measurable, Achievable, Relevant, and Time-bound) to define expectations. Break down large goals into smaller milestones to maintain engagement and momentum.
- **Conduct regular check-ins:** Schedule consistent one-on-one meetings to assess progress, address challenges, and adjust development plans as needed. Utilize digital dashboards or tracking tools to visualize progress.
- **Encourage self-assessment:** Employees should have the opportunity to reflect on their progress, compare it with supervisor evaluations, and take ownership of their development.
- **Provide timely feedback:** Offering real-time, constructive feedback ensures employees understand their progress and can make necessary improvements immediately.

How to Recognize Achievements

Acknowledging progress and celebrating success is crucial for reinforcing positive behaviors and maintaining motivation. Recognition doesn't have to be elaborate—what matters is that it is meaningful and aligned with individual preferences. Consider the following approaches:

- **Celebrate milestones and wins:** Recognize both small and significant achievements to maintain momentum. Simple gestures like a verbal acknowledgment, a team announcement, or a celebratory lunch can go a long way in reinforcing progress.
- **Personalize recognition:** Some employees appreciate public acknowledgment, while others prefer a private conversation or written appreciation. Tailor recognition to suit individual preferences.
- **Highlight specific contributions:** Instead of generic praise, link recognition to specific actions and their impact. For example, say, *"Your proactive approach in training new hires significantly improved onboarding efficiency, reducing ramp-up time by 20%."*
- **Tie achievements to broader goals:** Reinforce how individual and team successes contribute to the organization's mission and strategic objectives. Employees feel more engaged when they see the direct impact of their efforts.

Key Takeaways for Supervisors

- **Make progress measurable:** Establish clear, trackable goals and review them regularly to ensure alignment with development objectives.
- **Recognize early and often:** Frequent acknowledgment of achievements fosters motivation and reinforces positive behaviors.
- **Tailor recognition to individual needs:** Understand what motivates each team member and personalize recognition accordingly.
- **Link achievements to bigger goals:** Help employees see how their contributions fit into the larger mission, fostering a sense of purpose and engagement.

By implementing structured progress tracking and meaningful recognition, supervisors not only enhance individual development but also cultivate a high-performance team culture. When employees see that their growth is valued and celebrated, they become more invested in their roles, more engaged in their work, and more committed to the success of the organization.

Example in Action

Ava's supervisor, James, set quarterly performance goals for her and used biweekly check-ins to track progress. Each check-in focused on milestones achieved and areas that needed improvement. When Ava successfully launched a new client onboarding process ahead of schedule, James recognized her accomplishment with a team-wide announcement and a personal note of appreciation. This recognition boosted Ava's confidence and encouraged her to take on a more prominent leadership role in future projects.

Outcome

Measuring progress and recognizing achievements fosters a culture of accountability, motivation, and continuous improvement. When supervisors track progress, employees are more focused and goal-oriented. Recognition reinforces positive behaviors, increases employee engagement, and encourages sustained effort. Together, these practices drive performance, strengthen team morale, and promote long-term success for both employees and the organization.

The Long-Term Benefits of Team Development

Investing in team development yields both immediate and long-term rewards. As employees grow, the team becomes more capable, resilient, and aligned with organizational goals. Supervisors who prioritize development will notice fewer mistakes, more informed decision making, and higher levels of engagement. However, perhaps the most significant benefit is this: Your team will view you as a leader worth following.

Consider the long-term advantages of fostering a culture of continuous development:

- **Increased retention:** Employees are more likely to stay when they see clear opportunities for career growth.
- **Stronger team performance:** Well-developed teams make better decisions, adapt to challenges more effectively, and produce higher-quality work.

- **A sustainable leadership pipeline:** Today's learners become tomorrow's leaders. By investing in team development now, you're cultivating the next generation of leadership within your organization.

By making development a priority, supervisors lay the groundwork for sustained success. The impact of investing in people extends far beyond individual performance—it strengthens teams, enhances workplace culture, and drives long-term organizational growth.

Conclusion: Cultivating a Culture of Growth

Supporting team development is not just a leadership responsibility—it's a strategic advantage. The time, energy, and resources you invest in your team today will pay dividends for years to come. Teams that grow together perform better, innovate more, and remain more engaged.

Growth is not instantaneous. It's a process of nurturing potential, creating opportunities, and providing steady guidance. Every development conversation, every learning opportunity, and every moment of feedback contributes to the larger goal of building a high-performing, future-ready team.

Your legacy as a supervisor is not measured by how many tasks you complete but how many people you help develop. Each skill mastered, milestone reached, and promotion earned by your team members reflects your leadership in action. The most impactful leaders measure their success by the growth of their people.

By fostering a culture of continuous development, you are building a team that is not only stronger today but also prepared for the future. Employees who see their leaders invest in their growth are more likely to stay engaged, strive for excellence, and remain committed to the team. This commitment builds a lasting foundation of trust, loyalty, and shared purpose.

Take the long view. Plant the seeds of growth with intention and nurture them with encouragement, opportunity, and support. Over time, you will see your team members evolve into confident, skilled, and motivated contributors who drive the success of the team and the organization as a whole.

CHAPTER 8

Navigating Change and Uncertainty

Change is like a river—you can't stop it, but you can learn to navigate its currents.

I learned early in life that change is the only constant. Well, aside from death and taxes! Change is certainly ever-present in today's fast-paced work environment. It comes in many forms—new leadership, restructured teams, revised company goals, technological advancements, or process overhauls. Sometimes, change is anticipated, like the rollout of new software, while at other times, it comes suddenly and disruptively, such as a global pandemic or an unexpected shift in executive leadership. No matter how it arrives, change demands attention, adaptability, and skilled navigation.

As a supervisor, your role is not just to "deal" with change but to *lead* through it. Unlike individual contributors, who may experience change as something that happens *to them*, you must frame change as something that happens *with them* and *through them*. Your response to change will set the tone for your entire team. Will you react with confusion and anxiety, or will you demonstrate calmness, transparency, and confidence?

Leading through change requires more than simply communicating new directives from senior leadership. It demands empathy, strategic thinking, and the ability to balance operational stability with necessary adaptation. Employees often look to their supervisor for reassurance and clarity during turbulent times. If you appear unsteady, your team will feel unsteady too. Conversely, if you project resilience and optimism, your team will mirror that energy.

Before we dive into the practical tools and techniques, it's important to understand one core truth: Change isn't a single event—it's a process. It's not a switch you flip or a memo you send. It's a journey, and as a supervisor, you are the guide. This means you need to understand how people experience change, the psychology behind it, and how to address the common fears and uncertainties that come with it.

Navigating Change and Uncertainty: A Guide for New Supervisors

Change management represents one of the most crucial skills in a supervisor's toolkit. Prosci's research quantifies this importance starkly: Organizations that excel at change management are seven times more likely to meet project objectives to those with poor change management (Prosci 2024a). In addition, projects with effective change management are nearly five times more likely to stay on schedule and 1.5 times more likely to stay on budget (Prosci 2024b). For frontline supervisors, these statistics translate into daily realities that affect team performance, morale, and success.

Understanding the Psychology of Change

The human brain processes uncertainty as a threat, activating the same neural pathways as physical pain. This biological reality explains why even minor changes can trigger significant emotional responses from team members. Some will embrace change eagerly, while others will resist fiercely. As a supervisor, your success depends on understanding and working with these natural psychological responses rather than fighting against them.

The Four Pillars of Successful Change Leadership

Drawing on John Kotter's influential work on organizational change (Kotter 2012), combined with observations from experienced change leaders, we can identify four critical elements that determine change success:

Creating Urgency: The 70 Percent Rule

Change efforts often succeed when approximately 70 percent of an organization understands and supports an initiative. For supervisors, this means developing a compelling narrative about why change matters now. Rather than simply announcing changes, successful supervisors create understanding through stories, data, and personal connections. Share specific examples of how the status quo limits success and how change opens new possibilities. Make the case for change personal and relevant to each team member's experience.

Building Your Coalition: The 15 to 20 Percent Rule

Change initiatives require a critical mass of active supporters—often around 15 to 20 percent of the organization—to gain momentum. At the team level, this means identifying and empowering those who naturally embrace change. These early adopters become your change champions, helping peers see the benefits and possibilities of new approaches. Focus on building this support network early, as their influence often proves more powerful than any top-down directives.

Establishing Clear Vision: The 54 Percent Impact

A well-defined and inspiring vision can increase change success by as much as 54 percent. This means painting a vivid picture of what success looks like after the change. Help your team envision the practical benefits: more efficient processes, better customer outcomes, enhanced career opportunities. Make this vision tangible through specific examples and measurable outcomes. Your role is to transform abstract organizational goals into concrete realities your team can understand and embrace.

Communication Excellence: The 3.8× Multiplier

Change leaders have observed that effective communication can improve the odds of success by up to 3.8 times. This requires more than just regular updates—it demands creating genuine dialogue. Hold both team meetings and one-on-one conversations. Listen actively to concerns and address them honestly. Share what you know, acknowledge what you don't, and maintain consistent communication even when there's no new information to share.

The Supervisor as Change Navigator:
A Comprehensive Guide

PART ONE
Understanding Your Role in Organizational Change

Change cascades through organizations like water through a river system. While senior leaders determine the overall flow, supervisors like you control how that change actually reaches and affects team members. McKinsey's research reveals that frontline supervisors play a crucial role in change implementation, with significant impact on how employees experience and adopt organizational changes (McKinsey 2024). Organizations that effectively engage frontline employees in the change process are substantially more likely to implement innovations successfully and sustain transformation efforts.

Core Functions of a Change Navigator

Change is an inevitable part of any workplace, and supervisors play a critical role in guiding their teams through transitions effectively. Whether adapting to new company policies, shifting team structures, or implementing process improvements, supervisors must serve as change navigators—bridging the gap between leadership directives and team execution. To be successful in this role, supervisors must focus on three essential functions: translating vision into action, creating emotional safety, and maintaining forward momentum.

Building the Bridge: Translating Vision into Action

One of the primary responsibilities of a supervisor during change is transforming abstract organizational directives into clear, actionable steps for their team. Employees often struggle with broad, high-level initiatives that lack tangible application to their daily work. Supervisors must bridge this gap by breaking down changes into specific, manageable tasks that align with team operations.

For example, when a manufacturing company announced a shift to lean manufacturing principles, an effective supervisor ensured a smooth transition by:

- Creating visual process maps comparing current and future workflows
- Breaking down new procedures into daily task modifications to ease adoption
- Developing targeted skill-building exercises to reinforce key changes
- Establishing clear performance metrics to track progress and provide feedback

By translating the larger vision into digestible steps, supervisors empower employees to embrace change with clarity and confidence.

Creating Emotional Safety: The Psychology of Change

Change is not just a structural shift—it is an emotional experience. Uncertainty during organizational change can trigger stress and anxiety, as employees grapple with the unknown and fear their ability to adapt (Heifetz and Linsky 2002). As a supervisor, your role extends beyond managing tasks; you must create an environment where employees feel safe navigating uncertainty.

Harvard researchers refer to this as establishing a "psychological holding environment," where employees can express concerns, ask questions, and process the transition in a supportive setting (Harvard Kennedy School 2023). This concept—rooted in the work of psychoanalyst Donald Winnicott and adapted for organization leadership—underscores the important of providing structure, empathy, and space during turbulent periods.

Practical strategies to foster emotional safety include:

- Holding regular one-on-one check-ins to address individual concerns
- Creating open forums where team members can discuss challenges and uncertainties

- Establishing clear protocols for raising and resolving concerns to promote transparency
- Following through on commitments to build trust and demonstrate leadership reliability

When employees feel heard and supported, they are more likely to engage constructively with change rather than resist it.

Maintaining Forward Momentum: Balancing Stability and Progress

One of the biggest challenges of managing change is ensuring that day-to-day operations continue smoothly while new processes are being implemented. According to Prosci's research, teams with strong change management leadership are approximately seven times more likely to meet their transition objectives than those without structured guidance (Prosci 2024).

The key to maintaining momentum is striking a balance between stability and progress. Supervisors must reinforce the importance of continuity while keeping the team focused on the benefits of the upcoming transformation.

Effective strategies to sustain progress during change include:

- Setting incremental milestones to celebrate small wins and keep morale high
- Communicating the long-term benefits of change to maintain motivation
- Monitoring team workload to ensure changes do not overwhelm existing responsibilities
- Encouraging adaptability by framing challenges as opportunities for growth

Supervisors who successfully navigate change recognize that resistance is natural but not insurmountable. By providing structure, fostering emotional safety, and maintaining forward momentum, they help their teams adapt with resilience and confidence.

Change is not simply something to endure—it is an opportunity for transformation. With the right approach, supervisors can guide their teams through transitions in a way that strengthens trust, builds adaptability, and ultimately leads to greater success.

Balancing Three Critical Elements of Change Leadership

Clear and Transparent Communication

Effective communication is the foundation of successful change management. When employees are uncertain about their roles, responsibilities, or the organization's future, anxiety increases. In the absence of clear information, people often assume the worst, leading to decreased morale and greater resistance. As a supervisor, your role is to provide as much clarity and transparency as possible. The more employees understand what is happening, why it's happening, and how it affects them, the more confident and engaged they will be.

The key principles of clear communication during change include:

- **Clarity:** Explain the change in simple, direct language. Avoid jargon and ambiguous terms that might create confusion or distrust.
- **Transparency:** Share the reasons behind the change, particularly if it is due to external factors such as economic shifts or regulatory requirements. Providing context reassures employees that changes are intentional, not arbitrary.
- **Regular updates:** Keep your team informed at every stage of the change process. Even if there are no major updates, consistent communication prevents speculation and fosters trust.

During change, it is better to "over-communicate" than to risk employees feeling left in the dark. Repetition reinforces messages and reassures employees that leadership is actively managing the transition.

Providing Reassurance and Support

Change often triggers fear—fear of job security, loss of status, or an inability to keep up with new demands. Employees worry about whether they have the skills to adapt and, in some cases, whether their jobs are at risk. If these concerns go unaddressed, they can escalate into resistance and disengagement. Your role as a supervisor is to acknowledge these fears and provide the necessary reassurance and support to help your team navigate the transition with confidence.

Strategies for providing reassurance include:

- **Acknowledging concerns:** Instead of dismissing employee fears with statements like "You have nothing to worry about," validate their feelings by saying, "I understand that this change may feel unsettling. Let's talk about any specific concerns you have."
- **Framing change positively:** Rather than emphasizing what employees are losing, highlight what they stand to gain—whether it's new skills, career advancement, or increased influence in decision making.
- **Demonstrating empathy:** Different employees process change at different speeds. What excites one person may feel threatening to another. Be patient, listen actively, and tailor your support to each individual's needs.

Managing Resistance to Change

Even with clear communication and ample support, some employees will resist change. Resistance is not necessarily negative—it is a natural human response. People resist change when they feel a loss of control, when they fear failure, or when they do not understand why the change is necessary. Your job as a supervisor is not to eliminate resistance but to transform it into constructive engagement.

Key strategies for managing resistance include:

- **Listening first:** Before attempting to persuade someone, take the time to understand their concerns. Ask, "What about this change worries you?" or "What do you feel you are losing?" Once you identify the root cause of their resistance, you can address it more effectively.

- **Building ownership:** Employees resist change when they feel it is being forced upon them. Involve them in shaping how the change is implemented by giving them roles in decision making and problem solving.
- **Addressing the root cause of resistance:** Sometimes resistance stems not from the change itself, but from fear of the unknown or concerns about personal competency. Acknowledge these fears and provide the necessary resources or training to build confidence.

Rather than viewing resistance as defiance, treat it as valuable feedback. Ask yourself, "What about this change isn't clear or compelling to them?" Addressing resistance with patience and understanding will strengthen trust and lead to greater acceptance.

By balancing clear communication, emotional support, and proactive resistance management, supervisors can guide their teams through change successfully. Navigating change is not just about managing transitions—it's about leading people through uncertainty with confidence, clarity, and care.

PART TWO

Essential Components of Change Leadership

Building Change Readiness

Successful supervisors don't wait for change to happen before preparing their teams—they build a culture where adaptability is expected. According to McKinsey, organizations that take the time to identify and shift employee mindsets around change are four times more likely to achieve successful transformation outcomes (McKinsey 2021). By laying the groundwork early, supervisors ensure that when change does occur, employees are equipped to approach it with confidence rather than resistance.

A change-ready culture starts with normalizing adaptability. Teams should see process improvements and innovation as everyday aspects of work—not disruptions. Gallup research has shown that effective communication from leadership during periods of change significantly increases employee engagement and reduces burn out (Gallup 2023). Encouraging open discussions about potential improvements, recognizing creative problem solving, and embedding continuous learning into daily routines all contribute to a workforce that is more comfortable with change. Supervisors who foster an environment where questioning and rethinking processes are welcomed—rather than seen as a challenge to authority—create teams that can adjust more quickly when larger shifts occur.

Beyond cultural readiness, supervisors should focus on developing the skills necessary for change adaptation. Employees who are well-equipped with critical thinking, resilience, and collaborative problem-solving skills are more likely to navigate transitions smoothly. A study by Harvard found that leading organizations are expanding leadership development efforts beyond senior leaders to foster change-readiness across all levels of the workforce (Harvard Business Publishing 2023). Supervisors should integrate training and development opportunities that enhance these competencies, such as workshops on adaptability, coaching sessions focused on stress management, and cross-functional collaboration projects that expose employees to new ways of thinking.

Equally important is establishing a strong flow of information within the team. Change resistance often arises from uncertainty or misinformation, so supervisors must create structured channels for sharing updates, discussing industry trends, and gathering employee insights. Regular team briefings, open forums for discussing upcoming shifts, and clear feedback mechanisms ensure that employees feel informed and heard throughout the transition process. Supervisors who communicate proactively rather than reactively set the tone for a team that views change as an expected and manageable part of their work rather than an unexpected disruption.

Communication Frameworks for Change Leadership

Communication during change must be clear, consistent, and connected. Without a structured communication plan, employees may feel lost, leading to uncertainty, disengagement, or outright resistance. McKinsey's 3C Model—Clear, Consistent, and Connected—offers a framework for delivering effective change-related messages that drive understanding and alignment.

Clear Communication: The "What-Why-How" Framework

Supervisors must ensure that their messages are simple, direct, and free of ambiguity. Employees need clear answers to three fundamental questions:

- **What is changing?** Employees need to know exactly what will be different in their roles, processes, or responsibilities. For example, instead of saying, *"We're updating our customer service approach,"* a supervisor should specify: *"Starting next month, we'll implement a new customer service system that changes how we log and track inquiries."*
- **Why is it changing?** Employees are more likely to embrace change when they understand its purpose. Providing context, such as *"This change will reduce response time by 40% and improve customer satisfaction scores,"* helps employees see the bigger picture.
- **How will it happen?** Employees need a roadmap for implementation, including timelines and available support. *"Each team member will receive three days of training, with ongoing support from our IT team,"* ensures that employees know what to expect and how to prepare.

When supervisors frame change using this **What–Why–How** approach, employees gain clarity and feel less uncertain about what's ahead.

Consistent Communication: Establishing Rhythms for Updates

A single announcement is never enough. Supervisors must establish regular communication touchpoints to keep employees informed and engaged throughout the transition process. Change-related messages should be delivered through a mix of daily, weekly, and strategic updates:

- **Daily quick updates (5–10 minutes):** These brief check-ins help address immediate concerns, clarify new information, and reinforce key priorities.
- **Weekly team meetings (30–60 minutes):** A deeper review of progress, challenges, and necessary adjustments keeps the team aligned.

- **Monthly progress reviews:** These meetings assess the overall impact of the change and identify areas that need additional support or refinement.
- **Quarterly strategic alignments:** A high-level review ensures that long-term change efforts remain on track and integrated with broader company goals.

By making communication a regular and expected part of the process, supervisors eliminate uncertainty and ensure that employees stay engaged rather than feeling like change is something happening *to* them without their involvement.

Connected Communication: Linking Change to Purpose and Growth

Employees are more likely to embrace change when they see how it benefits them personally, contributes to team success, and aligns with the organization's broader mission. Supervisors should actively connect change initiatives to key motivators:

- **Individual growth:** *"This new system will help you develop more advanced customer service skills, positioning you for leadership opportunities."*
- **Team success:** *"By improving our workflow, we'll reduce delays and increase efficiency, making our jobs easier and our results stronger."*
- **Organizational goals:** *"This initiative aligns with our company's goal to improve customer satisfaction, which directly impacts our long-term success."*
- **Industry trends:** *"These changes keep us competitive in the marketplace, ensuring we stay ahead of evolving customer expectations."*

By linking change to tangible benefits, supervisors shift the conversation from one of resistance to one of opportunity. Employees who understand *why* a change matters and how it fits into their development and success are far more likely to engage with it positively.

PART THREE

Managing Change Implementation: Resistance Management

Research from McKinsey shows that 70 percent of change programs fail to achieve their goals, primarily due to employee resistance and lack of management support (McKinsey 2015). According to Prosci, resistant to change follow predictable patterns that can be systematically addressed through effective change management strategies (Prosci 2022). When organizations proactively anticipate and manage resistance, employees adapt more quickly and with less disruption, significantly improving overall project outcomes. In fact, Prosci's research indicates that when people are truly invested in change, it is 30 percent more likely to be sustained over time.

For supervisors, this means recognizing resistance as a natural human response—not a failure. By understanding its root causes and applying targeted strategies, they can transform potential barriers into opportunities for deeper engagement and long-term success

Understanding Resistance Types

Three primary forms of resistance commonly arise during change:

- **Logical resistance** is based on practical concerns about time, resources, or feasibility. Employees may worry that the change will disrupt workflow or require additional effort without clear benefits. Supervisors can address this by providing detailed implementation plans, allocating necessary resources, and offering structured training sessions.
- **Emotional resistance** stems from fear, uncertainty, or a perceived loss of control. Employees experiencing this type of resistance benefit from empathy, reassurance, and a supportive environment. Supervisors can create mentoring opportunities to help employees adjust and offer open discussions where concerns can be addressed constructively.

- **Personal resistance** is related to an employee's specific role, status, or job security. When change impacts an individual's position, they may resist due to fear of losing influence or career progression. Addressing this requires individual conversations, career development planning, and highlighting new growth opportunities created by the change.

Proactive Resistance Management

Early identification of resistance allows supervisors to intervene before it escalates. Common signs of resistance include changes in work patterns, increased questioning or skepticism, withdrawal from participation, and subtle non-compliance. Addressing resistance requires tailored strategies:

- For **logical resistance**, provide clear implementation roadmaps, data-driven justifications, and problem-solving sessions.
- For **emotional resistance**, increase communication, offer coaching, and reinforce positive aspects of the change.
- For **personal resistance**, engage employees in discussions about their future roles, provide skills training, and create opportunities for ownership in the new process.

By anticipating and managing resistance proactively, supervisors ensure smoother transitions and higher levels of team engagement during organizational change.

Team Morale Maintenance

Maintaining team morale during change is essential to keeping employees engaged, focused, and motivated. Research from MIT Sloan Management Review emphasizes that resilience and proactive engagement are more effectively sustained when organizations provide both stability and opportunity for growth—rather than placing the burden solely on individual employees to adapt (Fosslien and Duffy 2023). Supervisors play a central role in creating this balance by offering consistent communication, recognizing contributions, and supporting employee development. When team members feel secure yet challenged, they are more likely to remain resilient and embrace change as a path to growth rather than as a source of disruption.

Creating Stability

Change can create uncertainty, so establishing predictability in daily operations helps employees feel grounded. Supervisors should maintain regular team rhythms, provide clear communication patterns, and ensure dependable support systems. Consistent feedback loops help employees feel heard and supported, reinforcing their confidence in leadership.

Equally important is building trust through transparency. Employees appreciate honesty, even when uncertainty exists. Supervisors should openly share what they know about upcoming changes, admit when they don't have all the answers, and clearly explain decision-making processes. Following through on commitments builds credibility and reassures employees that they are in capable hands.

Fostering Growth

Periods of change provide unique opportunities for professional development. Supervisors should encourage employees to build new skills by offering targeted workshops, cross-training programs, leadership opportunities, and involvement in innovation projects. These initiatives help employees see change as a pathway to growth rather than an obstacle.

Recognition is another powerful tool for maintaining morale. Supervisors should celebrate small wins, acknowledge extra effort, share success stories, and reward employees for adapting to new challenges. Positive reinforcement fosters a culture of resilience and motivation, ensuring that teams remain engaged and proactive even in times of uncertainty.

By balancing stability and growth, supervisors create an environment where employees feel both supported and empowered, turning periods of change into opportunities for long-term success.

Measuring Success in Change Implementation

Success in change management is not just about completing a transition—it's about ensuring that the change is effective, sustainable, and aligned with organizational goals. To properly evaluate change implementation, supervisors should measure both hard metrics (tangible outcomes) and soft metrics (employee response and engagement). This dual approach allows leaders to assess both the technical success of the initiative and the human factors that influence long-term adoption and performance (Kaplan and Norton 1992; McKinsey & Company 2023b).

Hard Metrics: Measuring Tangible Outcomes

Supervisors must track objective performance indicators to assess whether the change has met its intended goals. These include:

- Completion of key project milestones on time and within budget
- Improvements in efficiency, such as streamlined workflows or reduced downtime
- Quality measurements, ensuring new processes maintain or enhance output
- Cost savings or financial benefits resulting from the change

This structured, outcomes-based approach is aligned with the Balanced Scorecard framework, which encourages monitoring of financial, operational, and strategic performance indicators to support sustained success (Kaplan and Norton 1992).

Soft Metrics: Evaluating Team Adaptation and Engagement

While hard metrics assess the technical side of change, soft metrics capture how well employees are adapting. These indicators help supervisors ensure that morale, communication, and collaboration remain strong throughout the transition. Key soft metrics include:

- Team engagement levels, assessed through feedback surveys and participation rates

- Effectiveness of communication, ensuring employees feel informed and involved
- Emergence of innovation, tracking whether employees proactively contribute ideas
- Collaboration quality, evaluating how well team members work together in the new system
- Speed of adaptation, monitoring how quickly employees embrace the change

According to McKinsey, organizations that monitor and respond to both hard and soft signals of change are more likely to sustain transformation over time and avoid common pitfalls such as disengagement and regression (McKinsey & Company 2023a).

Ensuring Sustainable Implementation

Successful change requires a structured, ongoing approach. Research indicates that organizations using a systematic implementation strategy achieve an 80 percent higher success rate than those without one.

- **Planning phase:** Develop detailed timelines, identify resource needs, map dependencies, and set checkpoints to guide progress.
- **Execution phase:** Monitor daily progress, address challenges promptly, adjust plans as needed, and maintain open communication.
- **Sustainability phase:** Embed new practices into company culture, document key learnings, share success stories, and plan for future improvements.

By combining rigorous measurement with structured implementation, supervisors ensure that change initiatives not only succeed but also deliver lasting benefits to the organization and its employees.

Remember: Successful change management isn't about avoiding all problems—it's about anticipating and managing them effectively. Your role as a supervisor is to guide your team through the process while maintaining both performance and morale.

Case Study: Navigating Digital Transformation at Regional Healthcare Services

The Challenge

When Sarah Chen was promoted to Supervisor of Patient Services at Regional Healthcare, she faced an immediate challenge: leading her team of 12 patient coordinators through the implementation of a new electronic health records (EHR) system. The change would fundamentally alter how her team handled patient scheduling, documentation, and communication.

Initial Situation

- Team had used the same paper-based system for 10+ years
- Several veteran team members expressed strong resistance
- 90-day implementation deadline
- No disruption to patient care allowed
- Team morale already strained from previous failed technology rollouts

Sarah's Systematic Approach

1. **Assessment and Preparation**
   First, Sarah conducted individual meetings with each team member to:
   - Understand their specific concerns
   - Assess technical comfort levels
   - Identify potential champions and resistors
   - Gather improvement suggestions for the new system

Key Discovery: The strongest resistance came from experienced staff who feared looking incompetent with new technology.

2. **Building Change Readiness**

   Sarah implemented a "Safe Learning" environment:
   - Created practice stations with the new system
   - Established peer support pairs (tech-savvy with tech-nervous)
   - Scheduled protected learning time during slower periods
   - Started daily 15-minute team huddles for updates and concerns

3. **Communication Strategy**

   She developed a clear communication framework:
   - Weekly e-mail updates on implementation progress
   - Daily huddle boards tracking training completion
   - Regular sharing of success stories
   - Open-door policy for concerns

4. **Managing Resistance**

   When Maria, a 15-year veteran, expressed strong resistance, Sarah:
   - Acknowledged her expertise with the current system
   - Asked for her input on training newer staff
   - Made her the "Process Quality Champion"
   - Provided extra one-on-one training support

Results After 90 Days

- 100 percent team completion of EHR training
- Zero disruption to patient scheduling
- 95 percent team proficiency with the new system
- Unexpected benefit: Maria became the team's unofficial EHR mentor
- Patient satisfaction scores maintained throughout transition
- Team morale improved as confidence grew

Key Lessons for New Supervisors

1. **Start with Understanding**
   Before implementing change, invest time in understanding individual team member perspectives and concerns.
2. **Create Safety for Learning**
   Establish an environment where mistakes are viewed as learning opportunities, not failures.
3. **Leverage Informal Leaders**
   Identify and engage influential team members who can help champion the change.
4. **Maintain Multiple Communication Channels**
   Different team members need different types of communication and support.
5. **Celebrate Progress**
   Regular recognition of small wins maintains momentum and builds confidence.

Long-Term Impact

Six months after implementation:

- Team became regional training center for the new system
- Three team members promoted to EHR specialists
- Department recognized for "Best Practice Implementation"
- Employee satisfaction scores increased by 40 percent

Why This Case Study Matters

This example demonstrates how effective change management requires:

- Clear understanding of team dynamics
- Systematic approach to implementation
- Flexible leadership style
- Focus on both task completion and team morale
- Recognition of individual needs and concerns

Conclusion: Leading Through Change—From Challenge to Opportunity

Effectively navigating change is a defining trait of successful supervision in today's dynamic workplace. Research consistently demonstrates that supervisors who master change management achieve significantly better outcomes. According to Prosci, organizations with excellent change management practices are up to seven times more likely to meet or exceed their objectives compared with those with poor change management (Prosci 2023).

Successful change leadership is built on three essential pillars:

- **Strategic communication:** Supervisors must translate organizational vision into practical steps, maintain transparent and frequent communication, and connect change initiatives to personal and team growth.
- **Emotional intelligence:** Managing the human side of change is just as critical as managing logistics. Studies from Harvard Business School highlights that emotionally intelligent leaders foster stronger collaboration, reduce stress, and improve employee performance. These leaders are better equipped to deliver feedback, coach teams, and create psychologically safe environments— leading to higher engagement and smoother change adoption (Landry 2019).
- **Systematic implementation:** A structured approach ensures sustainable success, balancing clear goals, flexible implementation strategies, continuous assessment, and real-time adjustments. Prosci emphasizes that applying a formal change management framework dramatically improves outcomes, particularly when resistance is anticipated and addressed proactively (Prosci 2023).

Mastering change management means more than just responding to transitions; it's about harnessing them as opportunities for growth, learning, and team development. Each change initiative provides a chance to strengthen team cohesion, build organizational capability, and refine your leadership effectiveness. As McKinsey and Company notes, organizations are over 40 percent more adaptable and significantly better equipped to handle future transitions (McKinsey & Company 2023b).

Ultimately, your success as a supervisor is not measured by avoiding change, but by how well you guide your team through it. By applying the principles outlined in this chapter, you can transform uncertainty into progress and lead your team toward meaningful, long-term success.

Now, hit those worksheets!

CHAPTER 9

Hiring Right: The Role of a Supervisor in Building a Team

Hiring is like matchmaking—you're looking for the perfect balance between skills, chemistry, and commitment.

Hiring is a delicate dance that requires patience, foresight, and an understanding of both the role you're filling and the people who will work alongside the new hire. For a first-time supervisor, hiring may seem like a straightforward task: post a job, interview candidates, and select the best one. But in reality, it's much more nuanced.

Every hire has the potential to shape your team's culture, performance, and morale. Hire the right person, and you create momentum—boosting energy, increasing productivity, and strengthening the team's overall chemistry. Hire the wrong person and the opposite can happen: decreased morale, missed deadlines, strained relationships, and an endless cycle of performance issues. This is why hiring is one of the most critical responsibilities of a supervisor. It's not just about filling a vacancy; it's about building a team that can consistently achieve goals and grow stronger over time.

This chapter is designed to demystify the hiring process and guide supervisors in making thoughtful, well-informed hiring decisions. We'll explore the strategies and tactics that experienced leaders use to attract, assess, and select top talent. We'll highlight the supervisor's role at each step of the hiring process, from defining the position to onboarding the new hire. As a supervisor, you play a pivotal role—not just in evaluating candidates but in selling the role, assessing for fit, and laying the groundwork for a smooth transition.

While HR departments often provide structural support for hiring, the supervisor must still take an active role in shaping the process. After all, no one understands the nuances of a team's needs better than the person who leads it. As a supervisor, you will need to assess technical skills, evaluate cultural fit, and gauge a candidate's long-term potential. It's more than just looking for the "best" person—it's about finding the *right* person for *your* team.

This chapter will provide you with the tools and mindset required to approach hiring like a seasoned leader. We will look at key concepts such as:

- Crafting a clear and accurate job description: How to ensure the job description attracts the right candidates and avoids attracting the wrong ones.
- Mastering the interview process: Strategies for conducting structured interviews that allow you to fairly and effectively compare candidates.
- Using behavioral interviewing techniques: Why "Tell me about a time when…" is one of the most powerful prompts in any interview.
- Avoiding bias in hiring: Recognizing and overcoming cognitive biases that can distort your decision-making process.
- Making the final decision with confidence: How to synthesize interview data, conduct effective reference checks, and choose the best candidate with conviction.
- Onboarding for success: Why hiring isn't over once a candidate says "yes" and how effective onboarding leads to long-term success.

This chapter is not a theoretical exercise—it's designed to be practical, actionable, and relevant to supervisors at any level. To bring these concepts to life, we'll walk through three illustrative case studies:

- XYZ Corp: A real-world example of how one company reduced turnover and boosted team performance by adopting a structured hiring approach.

- Google's approach to hiring: A look at how one of the world's most successful companies rethought the hiring process, focusing on skills over credentials.
- The retail hiring dilemma: A fictional but realistic case study of a retail store supervisor who faces the challenge of hiring during a peak season, balancing speed with quality.

These stories provide lessons for first-time supervisors on the importance of preparation, patience, and precision in the hiring process. By the end of this chapter, you will have a framework for hiring right—not just for the short term, but for the long-term success of your team.

When you approach hiring with intention, you're not just filling a role. You're shaping your team's future. Hiring right is not just about finding *a* person; it's about finding *the right* person who will help your team achieve its goals, support your leadership, and positively influence the team's dynamics. As you read on, you'll learn how to make that happen.

Let's get started.

The Philosophy of "Hire Slow, Fire Fast"

The philosophy of "hire slow, fire fast" is a cornerstone of effective team building and a guiding principle for successful supervisors. It reflects a fundamental truth about team dynamics: bringing the wrong person on board can cause long-term damage, while removing a poor fit swiftly can restore balance, productivity, and morale.

Supervisors are responsible for ensuring they have *the right person, in the right seat, doing the right thing*. This concept goes beyond hiring for skills alone. It's about matching the person's talents, temperament, and ambitions with the specific needs of the role and the broader team. This alignment leads to greater engagement, higher retention, and better overall performance.

The essence of "hire slow, fire fast" is patience on the front end and decisiveness on the back end. Taking the time to hire well ensures the right person is chosen for the right role, while quickly addressing a misaligned hire prevents further disruption to the team. Let's explore these two sides of the equation in detail.

Hiring Slow: Building a Deliberate Process for Lasting Success

Hiring slowly doesn't mean dragging your feet. It means being intentional, thorough, and thoughtful at every stage of the process. The goal is to make a decision that will stand the test of time, not just fill a vacancy as quickly as possible.

Many hiring mistakes are born out of urgency—when a supervisor is desperate to plug a gap. However, hiring in haste often leads to a misalignment of skills, expectations, and cultural fit. Supervisors who embrace a "hire slow" mindset understand that the cost of a bad hire is far greater than the inconvenience of a vacancy.

Steps for Hiring Slow

a. **Define Hiring Criteria**
   - What to do: Collaborate with your team to clearly define the essential skills, experience, and attributes required for success in the role. These criteria should be grounded in the needs of the team and the organization's long-term goals.
   - How to do it: Host team discussions or workshops to identify what qualities make an ideal hire. Prioritize traits such as problem-solving ability, adaptability, and EI alongside technical skills.
   - Example: At XYZ Corp, Sarah, a newly promoted marketing supervisor, asked her team to define the qualities they most valued in a new hire. They agreed that creativity, collaboration, and a commitment to innovation were essential for their fast-paced environment. By incorporating these traits into the hiring criteria, Sarah ensured the new hire would support the team's broader goals.

b. **Develop a Structured Process**
   - What to do: Create a multistep hiring process that allows for multiple perspectives, cross-functional input, and robust candidate evaluation.

- How to do it: Design a process that includes clear job descriptions, multiple interview rounds, skills assessments, and a final review meeting to synthesize feedback from stakeholders.
- Outcome: Sarah's well-defined process prevented "gut-feel" hiring decisions, which are often unreliable. By requiring structured interviews, she ensured that each candidate was evaluated consistently and objectively.

c. **Conduct Thorough Interviews**
- What to do: Use structured interviews, behavioral interview techniques, and multiple interview formats (e.g., phone screens, one-on-one interviews, and panel interviews).
- How to do it: Create a bank of standardized, role-specific questions based on past performance, problem solving, and teamwork. Each interviewer scores the candidate against these criteria, reducing bias.
- Outcome: When Alex applied for a senior marketing role at XYZ Corp, the interview process tested his technical knowledge, strategic thinking, and interpersonal skills. Thanks to the structured process, Sarah could identify his ability to deliver innovative marketing strategies while building positive relationships with teammates.

d. **Skills Assessments**
- What to do: Incorporate practical exercises into the hiring process. These could include role-playing customer service interactions, coding tests, writing exercises, or technical problem-solving challenges.
- How to do it: Tailor the exercise to reflect the core aspects of the role. For example, a project manager might be asked to create a project timeline, while a marketing specialist might be tasked with designing a campaign strategy.
- Outcome: During the skills assessment for a marketing role at XYZ Corp, Alex created a multichannel marketing campaign that exceeded expectations. His ability to integrate innovative solutions demonstrated his suitability for the role.

Firing Fast: Correcting Missteps with Decisiveness

Even the most thorough hiring process isn't foolproof. Occasionally, a hire who seems perfect on paper turns out to be a poor fit in practice. While it's tempting to "give them more time," this hesitation can cost your team lost productivity, diminished morale, and unnecessary stress.

Firing fast isn't about being heartless—it's about protecting your team and the organization's long-term success. If a supervisor recognizes that a hire is not meeting expectations despite coaching, it's best to act swiftly and decisively.

Steps for Firing Fast

a. **Early Intervention**
   - What to do: Identify performance issues quickly and communicate them directly. The earlier you spot and address a problem, the better the chance of course correction.
   - How to do it: Use regular one-on-one check-ins to review performance. Be specific about issues, provide support, and document every conversation.
   - Example: When Sarah noticed that one of her hires was missing deadlines and struggling with collaboration, she addressed it in their weekly check-in. Despite coaching and support, the performance issues persisted, prompting a decision to part ways.

b. **Set Clear Expectations**
   - What to do: Ensure that every employee understands their job responsibilities, success metrics, and performance expectations.
   - How to do it: Provide clear job descriptions, set expectations during onboarding, and use check-ins to reinforce clarity. Document performance expectations in writing so that there is no ambiguity.
   - Outcome: When Sarah had to let go of a misaligned hire, she had documentation of their repeated underperformance and unmet expectations. This made the termination process straightforward, fair, and legally defensible.

Balancing Expertise and Team Fit

A critical hiring question every supervisor must confront is: *"Do I hire for skills or fit?"* The answer is: *"Both."* While technical expertise can be taught, a person's attitude, EI, and capacity for growth are harder to train.

Evaluating Expertise

- What to do: Assess technical skills using real-world simulations and tests.
- How to do it: Ask candidates to complete assignments that reflect the demands of the job, like writing sample reports or solving real-world problems.
- Example: When hiring for a software engineering role, Sarah asked candidates to solve a coding problem live, demonstrating both technical ability and problem-solving skills.

Assessing Cultural Fit

- What to do: Hire people who align with your team's values, work style, and operating rhythm.
- How to do it: Assess cultural fit by inviting candidates to meet team members and asking questions that reveal their preferred work environment and communication style.
- Example: When Sarah hired Alex, she brought team members into the final interview, allowing them to assess how well he would integrate into the team.

The Supervisor's Role in Building the Team

The supervisor's role in hiring extends beyond selecting candidates. Supervisors are responsible for ensuring that every hire feels valued, included, and equipped to succeed. They must also ensure their team has a voice in the process, which increases buy-in and strengthens team culture.

Empowering Your Team

- What to do: Involve team members in the hiring process to build trust and ownership.
- How to do it: Allow employees to participate in interviews, provide feedback on candidates, and be part of the decision-making process.
- Outcome: When Sarah invited her team to interview Alex, they appreciated the opportunity to be heard, which increased buy-in once he was hired.

Onboarding and Integration

- What to do: Provide a well-structured onboarding process to set new hires up for success.
- How to do it: Use a 30-60-90 day onboarding plan, provide mentorship, and foster opportunities for early wins.
- Outcome: When Alex joined the team, Sarah paired him with an experienced mentor. By the end of his first 30 days, he had already made measurable contributions, boosting his confidence and solidifying his role on the team.

The Right Person, The Right Seat, The Right Role

When a supervisor embraces the "hire slow, fire fast" philosophy, they shift their mindset from short-term expediency to long-term growth. Every hire should be seen as a chance to elevate the team's potential, not just fill a gap. By focusing on finding *the right person, in the right seat, doing the right thing*, supervisors ensure that every person on the team is a valuable contributor.

This process requires patience, clarity, and decisiveness. Take your time to hire slow, and when necessary, fire fast. Every team member matters, and every hiring decision has a ripple effect on team cohesion, performance, and morale.

As a supervisor, remember this simple truth: *People don't quit companies, they quit managers*. Hire right, and you'll create a team that stays, grows, and thrives under your leadership.

Monitoring Performance

Hiring the right person is only half the battle—ensuring their continued growth and contribution is where a supervisor's real work begins. Monitoring performance is an ongoing process, not a one-time event. It requires setting clear expectations, providing regular feedback, and fostering a growth-oriented environment.

Supervisors must actively engage with their team members to ensure everyone understands what "good performance" looks like. Regular performance check-ins and formal reviews are essential tools for identifying both strengths and areas for development. This approach not only drives individual success but also strengthens the overall performance of the team.

When supervisors fail to monitor performance, small issues can fester into larger problems, ultimately affecting team morale, productivity, and turnover rates. Conversely, supervisors who prioritize continuous feedback and development create a culture of accountability, learning, and growth.

Historical Example: Google's Hiring Practices

Google is known for its meticulous hiring process, and for good reason. Their approach is built on the idea that great hires drive innovation and maintain a strong organizational culture. Google's hiring process is rigorous, ensuring candidates are assessed for both technical proficiency and cultural alignment.

Steps Taken

1. **Core Values-Driven Hiring**
   - What they do: Google prioritizes problem solving, adaptability, and collaborative skills in its hiring process. Rather than focusing solely on technical skills, the company seeks individuals

who can learn, unlearn, and relearn in a rapidly evolving environment.

- ○ Why it matters: This focus on adaptability allows Google to maintain a workforce that is ready to pivot as market needs change.

2. **Rigorous Interview Process**
   - ○ What they do: Candidates at Google undergo multiple rounds of interviews, each with a distinct focus. Interviews assess technical skills, problem-solving capabilities, and alignment with company values.
   - ○ Why it matters: Multiple rounds of interviews reduce the risk of hiring bias. Each round adds a layer of perspective, ensuring that a candidate is evaluated holistically.

3. **Panel Involvement**
   - ○ What they do: Google includes cross-functional teams in interviews to get diverse perspectives. Each panel member assesses candidates independently, and the final hiring decision is made collectively.
   - ○ Why it matters: This process ensures no single person has undue influence on the final decision, increasing the objectivity and fairness of the hiring process.

Outcomes

- **Increased retention:** Because of their meticulous process, Google's employees are more likely to stay long-term.
- **High employee satisfaction:** Employees hired through this process feel more connected to Google's mission, creating a shared sense of purpose and belonging.
- **Stronger company culture:** By hiring for both skill and cultural fit, Google preserves its values and maintains a collaborative, problem-solving environment.

Key Takeaways for Supervisors

1. **Hire slow, fire fast:** Supervisors must prioritize the "right person, right seat, right role" principle. A slow, deliberate hiring process

ensures high-quality hires, while decisive action to part ways with a poor fit protects team performance.

2. **Monitor and measure performance:** Regular feedback and performance check-ins prevent small problems from becoming major issues. Monitoring performance isn't about control—it's about ensuring every person on the team has clarity, support, and the opportunity to improve.

3. **Team involvement increases buy-in:** Involving team members in hiring decisions increases the likelihood of finding a great hire and builds team trust and cohesion.

4. **Onboarding and continuous support are critical:** Onboarding doesn't end after a week. Continuous support through coaching, mentorship, and feedback ensures new hires develop into high-performing contributors.

5. **Cultural fit matters as much as expertise:** Skills can be taught; cultural misalignment cannot. Supervisors should look for candidates who align with the team's values and dynamics.

6. **Data-driven decisions lead to better outcomes:** Use structured interviews, panel input, and quantitative performance reviews to eliminate bias and improve the quality of hiring decisions.

By taking a thoughtful, structured approach to hiring, onboarding, and performance monitoring, supervisors can build teams that deliver results, grow stronger with time, and create a positive, collaborative work environment. The role of a supervisor isn't just to hire—it's to *build* a team. Every decision to hire, fire, promote, or coach shapes the future of that team.

With the right person, in the right seat, doing the right thing, everything is possible.

Conclusion: Hire with Purpose, Lead with Confidence

Hiring is not just about filling an empty chair—it's about shaping the future of your team, your department, and your organization. As a supervisor, your hiring decisions have a ripple effect that extends far beyond the first 90 days of a new hire's tenure. Every hire is a chance to elevate your team's potential, strengthen its culture, and position it for long-term success.

The lessons from XYZ Corp, Google, and Jane's retail store illustrate a powerful truth: Great teams aren't found, they're built. Thoughtful hiring requires patience, structure, and a commitment to excellence. The supervisors in these case studies didn't settle for "good enough"—they aimed higher, and as a result, their teams thrived.

Here's the reality every supervisor must confront: It's better to have a temporary vacancy than a permanent liability. Rushing to fill a position may relieve short-term pressure, but it often creates long-term problems. A bad hire disrupts team morale, drains productivity, and forces supervisors to spend more time on corrective action than on strategic growth. The antidote to this cycle is simple but powerful: hire slow, fire fast.

Taking a slow, intentional approach to hiring doesn't mean dragging your feet. It means designing a process that allows you to fully evaluate candidates for both technical expertise and cultural alignment. It means engaging your team in the process, setting clear criteria, and leveraging multiple perspectives to make the most informed decision possible. It means resisting the temptation to hire the first "good enough" candidate in favor of the one who will thrive, grow, and make the team stronger.

But hiring doesn't end when the offer is accepted. Onboarding is the bridge between hiring and performance. The most thoughtful hiring process can still fail if onboarding is rushed or overlooked. Supervisors must ensure that new hires feel supported, understood, and equipped to succeed from Day 1. This means clear communication, regular check-ins, and providing a mentor or guide to help them navigate their new environment. The first 90 days of a new hire's experience are often a predictor of their long-term success.

Finally, don't forget the human element of hiring. It's easy to focus on resumes, qualifications, and interviews, but people are more than their skills. They bring their personalities, values, and aspirations to the workplace, and those attributes play a pivotal role in whether they'll fit the team. The right person, in the right seat, doing the right thing isn't just a slogan—it's a strategy for sustained success.

As you step into your role as a supervisor, remember that hiring is one of the most high-stakes decisions you will make. It requires patience, precision, and perspective. Take it seriously. Every person you hire either strengthens your team or weakens it. There is no middle ground. But with the tools, strategies, and principles laid out in this chapter, you are better equipped to make the right choice.

Your team is counting on you to get it right. And with the right process, you will.

Hire with purpose. Build with patience. Lead with confidence. Complete the worksheet.

CHAPTER 10

Understanding Performance Management and Accountability

Performance management: The art of turning feedback into fuel for growth, not fire for frustration.

Performance management is more than an annual review or a checklist of completed tasks. It's a continuous, dynamic process that shapes the way teams operate, grow, and achieve shared goals. For first-time supervisors, mastering performance management can feel like a balancing act—navigating the delicate line between support and scrutiny. But at its heart, effective performance management isn't about control; it's about clarity, communication, and commitment.

When done well, performance management transforms feedback into a catalyst for growth rather than a cause for conflict. It allows team members to see their progress, understand expectations, and take ownership of their development. For supervisors, it provides a structured approach to accountability, ensuring that goals are met, potential is unlocked, and underperformance is addressed before it festers.

For new supervisors, the pressure to "get it right" can be overwhelming. Unlike individual contributors who are evaluated on their own output, supervisors are measured by the collective performance of their team. This transition requires a shift in mindset—moving from "doing the work" to "driving the work." It means guiding others to success through clear goals, honest feedback, and unwavering accountability.

This chapter provides an in-depth look at the principles of performance management, offering practical strategies and real-world case studies to help supervisors foster high-performing teams. From establishing clear expectations and engaging in continuous feedback loops to conducting effective performance reviews, you will learn actionable steps to build a culture of accountability and growth.

Whether you're preparing for your first feedback conversation or facing your first tough performance discussion, this chapter will serve as your guide. By mastering these skills, you'll not only build a stronger team—you'll also earn the trust and respect of your employees as a leader who is committed to their growth and success.

Why Performance Management Matters

Performance management is often misunderstood as a one-time event—a dreaded performance review meeting scheduled at the end of the year. But successful supervisors know that true performance management is an ongoing process. It's the consistent rhythm of check-ins, feedback, goal setting, and course correction that keeps the team aligned, engaged, and motivated.

Here's why it matters:

1. Clarity of expectations: Employees perform better when they know what's expected of them. Vague instructions lead to inconsistent results, while clear objectives empower employees to focus and prioritize.

2. Continuous development: Employees want to grow, and performance management provides the structure for that growth. When you give employees specific, actionable feedback, they know exactly what to do to improve.

3. Accountability and ownership: Teams that operate without accountability fall apart. When supervisors make it clear that every action matters, employees begin to take ownership of their roles.

4. Retention and engagement: Employees don't leave companies; they leave bad supervisors. Performance management allows employees to feel seen, supported, and valued, reducing turnover and boosting morale.

5. Business impact: High-performing teams drive better results. Performance management ensures that everyone is working toward the same strategic goals, leading to higher productivity, better customer service, and stronger outcomes.

The Supervisor's Role in Performance Management

Supervisors are at the heart of performance management. As a new supervisor, you are now responsible for the success and growth of others. Your ability to set expectations, provide feedback, and address issues head-on will define your effectiveness as a leader.

Your role in performance management includes the following key responsibilities:

1. Goal setter: You must define clear, measurable goals for your team members. Goals should be Specific, Measurable, Achievable, Relevant, and Time-bound (SMART) to ensure clarity.
2. Coach and mentor: Gone are the days of "bosses" who bark orders and expect results. Today's supervisors must coach their employees, guiding them toward growth, encouraging learning, and helping them overcome obstacles.
3. Accountability partner: When goals aren't met, supervisors must hold team members accountable. Accountability isn't about punishment; it's about fairness, transparency, and integrity.
4. Feedback giver: Feedback should be a gift, not a grievance. Supervisors should strive to create an environment where feedback is frequent, constructive, and focused on growth—not blame.
5. Performance reviewer: The formal review process should be seen as a culmination of ongoing feedback, not a surprise meeting. Supervisors must document and discuss performance trends, successes, and areas for improvement.

The Key Elements of a Strong Performance Management System

To be effective at performance management, supervisors must understand the essential components of a strong system. These components serve as the foundation for effective supervision.

1. Goal Setting and Alignment
   - Set clear, strategic goals for both individual employees and the team as a whole.

- Align individual goals with the organization's larger objectives.
- Review and adjust goals regularly as priorities shift.

2. Ongoing Feedback and Coaching
   - Establish a feedback loop where employees receive regular, informal feedback.
   - Use a "feed-forward" approach, where feedback is framed as guidance for the future, not criticism of the past.
   - Encourage self-assessment and reflection from employees during one-on-ones.

3. Regular Check-ins and One-on-One Meetings
   - Schedule weekly, biweekly, or monthly one-on-ones with employees.
   - Discuss workload, progress on goals, and any obstacles that need to be addressed.
   - Ask open-ended questions to encourage dialogue, such as "What's one thing I can do to support you better this week?"

4. Accountability and consequences
   - Set clear standards for accountability and communicate them to your team.
   - When performance issues arise, address them quickly and respectfully.
   - Use a progressive approach to discipline, starting with coaching and support before moving to formal actions.

5. Formal Performance Reviews
   - Conduct mid-year and end-of-year performance reviews.
   - Use data and documented examples to support your evaluation.
   - Involve employees in the process by allowing them to complete a self-assessment.

Common Challenges for New Supervisors

New supervisors often face unique challenges in performance management. Here's how to address some of the most common obstacles:

1. Avoiding Difficult Conversations
   - *The challenge*: New supervisors may hesitate to give constructive feedback, fearing it will damage relationships.

- *Solution*: Reframe feedback as a way to support growth, not as a "gotcha" moment. Plan your words carefully and lead with empathy.

2. Setting Unrealistic Expectations
   - *The challenge*: Supervisors sometimes set goals that are too ambitious or unclear.
   - *Solution*: Follow the SMART goal-setting framework. Goals should be specific, clear, and achievable within a realistic timeframe.

3. Relying on Annual Reviews Alone
   - *The challenge*: If feedback is only given during formal reviews, employees will feel blindsided.
   - *Solution*: Establish an ongoing feedback culture where check-ins and coaching sessions are a routine part of work.

4. Failing to Address Poor Performance
   - *The challenge*: Supervisors may avoid difficult conversations about underperformance.
   - *Solution*: Tackle performance issues early and frame them as opportunities for growth. Use documentation to track progress and improvement.

5. Lack of Documentation
   - *The challenge*: Without proper documentation, supervisors may struggle to support performance decisions.
   - *Solution*: Keep a log of employee performance, including successes, challenges, and any critical feedback. This will provide clear evidence during formal reviews.

Performance management isn't just a process—it's a philosophy. It's a way of leading that prioritizes growth, accountability, and continuous improvement. For first-time supervisors, learning to manage performance is one of the most essential leadership skills to master. It requires patience, courage, and consistency.

By using the principles in this chapter, you'll be equipped to set clear expectations, deliver honest feedback, and create an environment of trust and accountability. Remember, performance management isn't something you "do to" employees—it's something you do *with* them. It's a partnership where the supervisor and the employee work together to achieve mutual success.

When done well, performance management creates a win–win scenario: employees grow, teams thrive, and you, as a supervisor, build a legacy of leadership. So lean into the process. Turn feedback into fuel, not fire. And watch your team—and your own career—soar.

Performance management isn't about "catching mistakes"—it's about *creating opportunities for growth*. Stay consistent, stay clear, and most importantly, stay committed.

The Performance Review Process

Performance reviews are not singular events—they're part of an ongoing dialogue between supervisors and employees. Effective reviews create a shared understanding of past performance, future goals, and actionable next steps. For first-time supervisors, mastering this process requires preparation, empathy, and the ability to communicate with both honesty and tact.

There are two key components of the performance review process: ongoing performance management and formal performance reviews. By mastering both, supervisors can avoid the "once-a-year surprise" and foster an environment of continuous growth and accountability.

Ongoing Performance Management

Performance management is not a once-a-year event—it requires continuous interaction to promote growth and address challenges in real time. Regular check-ins and feedback loops prevent misalignment, provide timely course correction, and reduce the stress and anxiety that often accompany formal reviews.

Regular Check-Ins

Frequent, informal discussions allow supervisors to provide timely feedback, uncover potential roadblocks, and offer support when needed. Instead of waiting for the next formal review, supervisors should have ongoing conversations with their team members.

How to Implement Check-Ins Effectively

- Schedule consistent one-on-ones (weekly, biweekly, or monthly, depending on team needs).
- Keep the agenda flexible to allow employees to raise their own concerns.
- Use open-ended questions to spark dialogue, such as:
  - *"What obstacles are you facing right now?"*
  - *"How can I support you this week?"*
  - *"What's one thing you'd like to achieve before our next check-in?"*
  - *"What support do you need from me?"*

Example: At Tech Solutions Inc., Sarah conducted one-on-one meetings every 2 weeks with her direct reports. She used these sessions to understand her team's challenges, provide ongoing feedback, and recognize small wins.

Outcome: Employees felt valued, and the consistent feedback loop reduced anxiety about formal reviews. Knowing where they stood at all times increased engagement and created a sense of security for the team.

Feedback Loop

A continuous cycle of positive reinforcement and constructive feedback creates a growth-oriented culture. The goal is not only to correct poor performance but also to recognize and amplify good performance.

Best Practices for a Feedback Loop

- Use the *Start, Stop, Continue* framework:
  - Start doing: New behaviors employees should adopt
  - Stop doing: Counterproductive behaviors that need to end
  - Continue doing: Positive behaviors that should be reinforced
- Provide timely feedback—don't wait for a scheduled review.
- Make feedback specific, not general. For example, instead of "Great job on the report," say, "I appreciate the way you included specific examples in the report—it made your key points much clearer."

Outcome: By highlighting individual contributions and offering clear suggestions for improvement, Sarah boosted her team's motivation and productivity. The process was collaborative, not punitive, and her employees felt empowered to make changes without feeling criticized.

Formal Performance Reviews

While ongoing check-ins keep employees on track, formal reviews offer an opportunity to evaluate progress, set goals, and foster accountability. These reviews are a chance to "zoom out" and look at the big picture of an employee's performance.

Setting Measurable Goals

Goals drive employee motivation and provide a clear direction for effort. Without clear goals, employees can become disengaged or misaligned with team priorities.

How to Set Goals Effectively

- Use the SMART goal-setting framework:
  - Specific: What exactly do you want the employee to achieve?
  - Measurable: How will success be measured?
  - Achievable: Is the goal realistic, given resources and capacity?
  - Relevant: Does the goal align with team and organizational priorities?
  - Time-bound: What is the deadline for completion?

Example: Alan Mulally's turnaround of Ford Motor Company involved clear, measurable goals for each division. His insistence on open communication and data-driven accountability resulted in a dramatic cultural shift at Ford, driving alignment and improved performance.

Action Plans for Improvement

When performance issues arise, supervisors must offer a clear pathway for improvement. This is especially critical when dealing with underperformance. An action plan outlines the steps an employee should take, the support they will receive, and the timeframe for improvement.

How to Create an Action Plan

1. Identify the gap: Clearly articulate what performance standard is not being met.
2. Define the solution: List the specific actions the employee should take to improve.
3. Provide support: Identify the training, coaching, or tools the employee needs.
4. Set milestones: Break the plan into small, measurable steps.
5. Document the plan: Create a written document that both you and the employee can reference.

Outcome: Sarah helped employees struggling with specific tasks by offering additional training and breaking down improvement into smaller, achievable milestones. The result? Higher performance, fewer mistakes, and greater employee confidence.

Documenting and Tracking Performance

Documentation is critical for performance reviews. Without records, it's difficult to provide concrete feedback or justify performance-based decisions, such as promotions, raises, or terminations.

How to Document Performance

- Use a simple system (like a performance journal) to record feedback, milestones, and issues as they arise.
- Track both positive and negative performance—don't only document "problem cases."
- Use specific examples in your documentation, noting what happened, when it happened, and why it matters.

Tip: Use technology to simplify the process. Work with your HR team to use your organization's performance management software.

Accountability Without Micromanagement

Accountability should not feel like "watching over shoulders." It should feel like empowerment. Supervisors should establish a culture of ownership, where team members take responsibility for their own work and outcomes.

Empowering Your Team

Empowerment fosters a sense of ownership and accountability. It sends the message, "I trust you," which increases motivation, engagement, and performance.

How to Empower Your Team

- Set clear expectations: Employees cannot be accountable for something they don't understand. Provide crystal-clear guidance on goals, deadlines, and responsibilities.
- Encourage self-reflection: Invite employees to reflect on their own performance. Self-assessment builds self-awareness and helps employees take ownership of their growth.

Example: Tom, a new sales manager at GreenTech Corp., collaborated with his team to set clear sales targets and engagement benchmarks. **Outcome**: Employees at GreenTech began reflecting on their performance, which boosted self-awareness and accountability.

Avoiding Micromanagement

Micromanagement kills motivation and creativity. It sends the message, "I don't trust you." Instead, focus on guiding employees, not controlling them.

How to Avoid Micromanagement

- Delegate and trust: Assign responsibility and let employees figure out their own process for achieving results.

- Focus on outcomes, not processes: Let go of "how" work is done as long as deadlines and goals are met.
- Use milestone check-ins: Set milestone check-ins to gauge progress without being overbearing.

Example: At Tech Solutions Inc., Sarah delegated tasks to team members and set milestone check-ins. Her team knew she would be available for support if needed, but they had the autonomy to complete their work.

Fostering a Culture of Accountability

Accountability doesn't happen by accident—it must be built into the team culture. When every team member feels responsible for their role, performance naturally improves.

How to Build a Culture of Accountability

- Recognize effort and achievement: Public recognition motivates employees to repeat positive behaviors.
- Address accountability issues early: Don't let small issues grow into big problems. Tackle them head-on.
- Use team huddles to reaffirm accountability: In team meetings, review shared goals and ask each person to state their current priorities.

Example: Sarah publicly acknowledged team achievements, like hitting project deadlines early or surpassing quality benchmarks.
Outcome: By consistently recognizing effort and addressing issues early, Sarah created a team culture where accountability was a shared responsibility.

Performance management is not a one-time task—it's an ongoing process of goal setting, feedback, and accountability. It requires supervisors to be coaches, mentors, and leaders all at once. By mastering regular check-ins, creating clear action plans, and fostering a culture of empowerment, first-time supervisors can elevate their teams and establish themselves as respected leaders.

When you focus on empowerment, not control—on growth, not punishment—performance management becomes a powerful tool for transformation. By turning feedback into fuel, you'll not only improve your team's performance but also build a legacy of leadership that extends far beyond your current role.

The best supervisors don't "manage performance"—they inspire it. Focus on clarity, accountability, and growth, and you'll turn your team into a high-performing powerhouse.

Case Study 1: Ford Motor Company's Turnaround

Industry: Automotive
Timeframe: Early 2000s
Key Player: CEO Alan Mulally

In the early 2000s, Ford Motor Company faced declining market share, mounting financial losses, and internal dysfunction. Morale was low, silos were entrenched, and accountability was inconsistent. To address these challenges, Ford hired Alan Mulally as CEO, a leader known for his transformative work at Boeing.

Steps Taken

1. **Assessment of leadership practices**: Mulally conducted a full review of Ford's leadership culture. He quickly identified issues with finger-pointing, poor communication, and a lack of shared goals across divisions.
2. **Establishment of a Business Plan Review (BPR) process**: Mulally introduced weekly "Business Plan Review" (BPR) meetings where senior leaders were required to present the status of their key objectives. Each leader displayed their results using a color-coded system: green for "on track," yellow for "at risk," and red for "off track."
3. **Promotion of transparency and accountability**: Leaders were encouraged to be honest about problems and seek collaborative

solutions rather than hiding issues. Those who used "red" status were supported, not punished, fostering a culture of openness and problem solving.

4. **Clear, measurable goals**: Mulally implemented a clear set of company-wide goals focused on "One Ford"—a unified strategy that aligned all business units under one global vision.

Outcomes

- **Return to profitability**: Ford became one of the only U.S. automakers to avoid bankruptcy during the 2008 financial crisis, posting a $2.7 billion profit in 2009.
- **Collaborative leadership**: The BPR process created a transparent, solutions-focused leadership environment. Executives who had been competitors began to operate as one team.
- **Employee empowerment**: Employees at all levels were encouraged to share ideas, identify challenges, and seek help without fear of retribution.

Lesson Learned

Clear expectations, consistent feedback, and empowerment drive accountability and innovation. Mulally's approach demonstrated that transparency and accountability don't just improve performance—they transform organizational culture.

Case Study 2: GreenTech Corp's Sales Team Beta

Industry: Clean Energy Sales
Scenario: Turnaround of an underperforming sales team
Key Player: Sales Manager Tom

GreenTech's Sales Team Beta was in trouble. They had missed three consecutive quarterly sales targets, and team morale had hit an all-time low. The previous manager had focused heavily on tracking every move the sales reps made, leading to micromanagement, distrust, and disengagement. When Tom was hired as the new Sales Manager, he recognized that to get the team back on track, he needed to rebuild trust, foster a culture of ownership, and introduce a clear, performance-driven management system.

Steps Taken

1. **Individual assessments**: Tom began by holding one-on-one meetings with each sales rep. He asked open-ended questions to understand their personal and professional challenges. For example, he asked, "What's the biggest hurdle you face when trying to close a sale?" and "How do you think we could improve the sales process?"
2. **Collaborative goal setting**: Instead of issuing arbitrary quotas, Tom involved his team in setting shared sales targets. This approach gave employees a sense of ownership and increased buy-in for the targets.
3. **Introduction of weekly progress reviews**: Each Monday, the team met to review sales performance, identify barriers, and discuss strategy adjustments. Tom emphasized that these reviews were not about blame but about problem solving.
4. **Self-assessments and peer feedback**: Team members completed self-assessments every month, rating their own performance and providing constructive feedback to peers. This process improved self-awareness and peer-to-peer accountability.
5. **Recognition and celebration of success**: During company-wide meetings, Tom publicly acknowledged team successes. Individual sales reps who hit their targets were highlighted, and significant sales wins were celebrated.

Outcomes

- **Sales turnaround**: Within two quarters, Sales Team Beta exceeded its target for the first time in over a year. By the end of the fiscal year, they had met 110 percent of their annual sales goal.

- **Improved team morale:** By replacing micromanagement with empowerment, Tom fostered a high-trust environment. Team members felt heard, respected, and supported.
- **Sustainable accountability:** Through self-assessments and peer feedback, employees became active participants in their own development, holding each other accountable for results.

Lesson Learned

Empowering employees through collaboration and accountability fosters team success. By shifting from "manager control" to "employee ownership," Tom's team took charge of their own performance. Employees work harder and smarter when they have a sense of control and clear, achievable goals.

Case Study 3: Riverside Hospitality's Front Desk Transformation

Industry: Hospitality and Customer Service
Scenario: Customer service improvement at a hotel's front desk
Key Player: Front Desk Supervisor Emma

When Emma took over as supervisor of the front desk at Riverside Hospitality, she faced two major issues: excessive guest complaints and inconsistent service quality. Customer satisfaction ratings had dropped from 85 to 62 percent in a year, and turnover among front desk staff was high. Emma knew she had to reframe performance management as a growth opportunity, not a punitive process.

Steps Taken

1. **Root cause analysis:** Emma identified patterns in guest complaints (long wait times, unfriendly staff, and errors in booking) and discussed these issues with her team. She discovered that staff felt unsupported and undertrained.

2. **Training and development plan**: Emma launched a training program that included role-playing guest interactions and handling difficult conversations. Employees received feedback in real-time and were encouraged to reflect on their progress.

3. **Daily "Pre-Shift Huddles"**: Every morning, Emma gathered the team for a quick 10-minute huddle. The team discussed key priorities for the day and addressed potential customer service challenges.

4. **Feedback loops with staff**: Emma conducted monthly one-on-one feedback sessions with each employee, focusing on growth rather than fault-finding. Employees were encouraged to reflect on their own performance, and Emma supported them with personalized development plans.

5. **Customer recognition program**: To foster a culture of accountability and pride, Emma created a customer recognition wall where guests could leave positive feedback for specific front desk employees. This public recognition had a profound impact on morale.

Outcomes

- **Service quality improvement**: Customer satisfaction ratings improved from 62 to 90 percent within 6 months.
- **Lower employee turnover**: Turnover among front desk staff dropped from 40 to 15 percent within a year.
- **Employee development**: The training program improved staff confidence and reduced service errors.

Lesson Learned

Accountability doesn't have to be punitive. When supervisors combine feedback, training, and recognition, they create a learning culture. By giving employees the tools and support they need to succeed, performance issues are resolved faster and employee engagement soars.

Key Takeaways

Each case study highlights essential lessons about performance management, feedback, and accountability. Here are the key takeaways for supervisors:

1. Assessment is key: Before making changes, assess the root causes of underperformance. Are employees unclear on expectations? Do they lack the skills to succeed? Is there a trust issue? Assessment is the foundation for improvement.
2. Clear expectations matter: Employees must understand what success looks like. This requires clear, measurable, and achievable goals that are aligned with team objectives.
3. Regular feedback promotes growth: Feedback should not be an annual event. Continuous feedback keeps employees on track, reduces anxiety, and supports growth.
4. Empowerment drives engagement: When employees have a voice in setting goals, reflecting on performance, and proposing solutions, they become more engaged.
5. Celebrate achievements: Recognition is one of the most powerful drivers of employee engagement. Celebrate wins, both big and small, to keep your team motivated.
6. Accountability should be supportive, not punitive: Accountability works best when it is built on trust. Employees are more willing to improve if they feel supported, not judged.

Performance management is about people, not processes. The leaders who inspire the most growth are those who create an environment of trust, empowerment, and continuous learning. These case studies show that small, intentional changes can lead to big results. As a supervisor, your ability to assess, align, support, and recognize your employees will define your success as a leader.

Accountability isn't about catching mistakes—it's about creating opportunities for improvement. When you focus on clarity, empowerment, and trust, you'll transform your team from followers into partners in progress.

Conclusion

Performance management isn't just about tracking metrics or conducting annual reviews—it's about shaping a culture where growth, accountability, and continuous improvement are the norm. It's about giving people the clarity they need to succeed, the feedback they need to grow, and the recognition they need to stay engaged.

Through the lessons from Ford Motor Company, GreenTech, and Riverside Hospitality, we've seen how clear expectations, open communication, and accountability can turn struggling teams into high-performing powerhouses. When supervisors shift from managing tasks to driving growth, they create an environment where performance is a shared responsibility.

For first-time supervisors, this transformation requires a shift in mindset. It means letting go of control and embracing empowerment. It means replacing vague demands with clear goals and using feedback not as a weapon, but as a gift. This chapter has equipped you with the tools to do just that:

- Set clear, SMART goals that leave no room for confusion.
- Create ongoing feedback loops so performance issues are caught early—not at the year-end review.
- Foster a culture of accountability where employees own their results and seek solutions before problems escalate.

Most importantly, remember that performance management is a process, not a one-time event. It's a continuous dialogue between supervisor and employee. When done well, it builds trust, strengthens relationships, and fuels sustainable success.

As a supervisor, you are no longer just responsible for your own output—you are responsible for helping others thrive. Your legacy as a leader will be measured not by what you achieve alone, but by what your team achieves under your guidance.

The best supervisors don't wait for performance to slip—they shape it, inspire it, and sustain it every day. Manage with purpose, coach with empathy, and hold your team (and yourself) accountable for results. Do that, and you won't just meet expectations—you'll exceed them.

CHAPTER 11

Leading with Empathy and Allowing Space to Fail

They say failure is the best teacher—but only if you're willing to be a student. So if you find me burning dinner while flipping through a leadership book, just know I'm mastering two lessons at once: patience and perspective.

Empathy and the acceptance of failure are two vital components for effective leadership. For first-time supervisors, these concepts can feel foreign or even counterintuitive. After all, many supervisors were promoted because they consistently "got it right" in their previous roles as individual contributors. But leadership requires a shift in mindset: It's no longer about how well *you* perform the task—it's about how well *your team* performs it. This means creating an environment where mistakes are not just tolerated but viewed as essential steps toward growth and innovation.

The pressure to "get everything right" can weigh heavily on new supervisors. But perfectionism, if left unchecked, stifles creativity, discourages initiative, and creates an atmosphere of fear rather than trust. That's why the most effective supervisors prioritize empathy and build a "place to fail"—a space where employees feel safe taking calculated risks, making mistakes, and learning from them without the fear of retribution.

Empathy and failure are a leadership duo that work hand in hand. Empathy allows you to see the human behind the mistake, understand their perspective, and recognize that the road to mastery is often paved with errors. When employees know their supervisor understands and supports them, they're more willing to take initiative. This is where true growth happens—not in the comfort zone but at the edge of capability.

This chapter delves into these two powerful leadership principles, exploring how empathy fuels growth, how to build a safe space for failure, and how to use mistakes as opportunities for development. Drawing on historical leadership examples, practical case studies, and fictional anecdotes, you'll see how these concepts play out in real-life supervisory roles. You'll also learn strategies to apply them with your team. By the end of this chapter, you'll not only understand why empathy and failure are essential to leadership but also have the tools to cultivate both in your workplace.

The Shifting Role of a Supervisor: From "Fixer" to "Facilitator"

When you were an individual contributor, your job was simple (though not always easy): complete tasks, solve problems, and meet deadlines. But as a supervisor, your job shifts from *doing the work* to *enabling others to do it well.* This shift often comes with growing pains. It requires patience, letting go of control, and resisting the urge to "fix" every problem yourself.

Here's the hard truth: If your team never fails, it may be because you're doing too much of their work for them. A supervisor who solves every problem robs their team of the chance to develop problem-solving skills. Worse, it signals to employees that failure is *not an option.*

Your role as a supervisor is not to prevent mistakes—it's to *prepare for them.* Mistakes will happen. And when they do, how you respond will define your leadership. If you respond with blame, anger, or micromanagement, you'll cultivate a team of risk-averse employees who never go beyond the bare minimum. If you respond with curiosity, empathy, and support, you'll create a culture of experimentation, growth, and continuous improvement.

Supervisors often feel the need to "look competent" in front of their teams. But paradoxically, the more you allow others to fail (and learn), the more competent you'll appear. Your confidence comes not from having all the answers but from creating an environment where your team feels empowered to *find* the answers.

Creating a Safe Space to Fail

For decades, many workplaces adhered to a rigid, failure-averse mindset, where mistakes were met with punishment or blame. Employees were expected to get everything right the first time, creating environments where innovation stalled, risks were avoided, and people hesitated to take ownership of new challenges. However, modern research shows that allowing employees to fail—and learn from those failures—is a critical ingredient in fostering high-performing teams.

Consider the case of Google's Project Aristotle, an extensive study designed to uncover what made the company's most successful teams thrive. Researchers found that psychological safety—the belief that team members could take risks, ask questions, and make mistakes without fear of humiliation—was the single most important factor in predicting a team's effectiveness. Teams that had high psychological safety were more likely to innovate, collaborate effectively, and find creative solutions to problems, while teams that lacked it struggled with engagement and productivity.

Google wasn't the first to embrace this mindset. Toyota's Kaizen philosophy, which prioritizes continuous improvement, actively encourages employees to point out inefficiencies, even if doing so means acknowledging a mistake. Instead of punishing errors, Toyota celebrates employees who identify problems as catalysts for organizational learning. As a result, Toyota has built a culture where employees feel empowered to experiment and refine processes without fear of retribution.

For supervisors, fostering this type of culture means shifting the perception of failure from something to be avoided to something that drives growth. It involves leading by example—acknowledging your own mistakes, framing failures as learning experiences, and encouraging open discussions about challenges without placing blame. When employees know that mistakes won't derail their careers, they are more likely to take calculated risks, develop creative solutions, and continuously improve.

The key takeaway is this: great teams don't avoid failure; they leverage it as a steppingstone for success. Supervisors who create a psychologically safe environment will cultivate a workforce that is resilient, innovative, and unafraid to take on new challenges.

The Key Elements of a Failure-Friendly Culture

Framing Failure as a Learning Opportunity

Supervisors must set the tone that failure is not a reflection of incompetence but an opportunity to learn and improve. When mistakes occur, rather than asking, *"Who is responsible?"* shift the focus to *"What can we learn from this?"* By encouraging this perspective, leaders create an environment where employees feel safe experimenting and refining their approaches without fear of repercussions.

Encouraging Risk-Taking

Innovation cannot thrive in an environment where people fear the consequences of failure. Supervisors should actively encourage team members to step outside their comfort zones and pursue new challenges. By setting realistic expectations and emphasizing progress over perfection, leaders can help employees develop confidence in their abilities while reducing the stigma around making mistakes.

Providing Constructive Feedback

Failure is only valuable when it leads to improvement. Supervisors must provide timely, constructive feedback that helps employees understand what went wrong and how they can adjust moving forward. This should be done in a supportive, solution-oriented manner rather than in a way that discourages future risk-taking. The situation–behavior–impact (SBI) model is a useful framework for delivering feedback that is clear, objective, and actionable.

Celebrating Resilience and Adaptability

Instead of solely celebrating successes, acknowledge resilience and perseverance in the face of challenges. Recognizing employees for their ability to bounce back and apply lessons learned fosters a culture of continuous improvement. Publicly highlighting stories of growth through failure helps normalize the idea that setbacks are a natural part of professional development.

The Importance of Allowing Space for Failure

Encouraging employees to embrace failure as a learning tool is crucial for fostering innovation, resilience, and continuous growth. When employees feel safe to experiment and take risks, they develop problem-solving skills, increase creativity, and build confidence in their abilities.

Encouraging Innovation and Creativity

Innovation flourishes when employees are given the freedom to experiment, even if failure is a possibility. Google's "20% time" policy is a prime example of this principle in action. Employees are encouraged to dedicate 20 percent of their time to passion projects unrelated to their core responsibilities. While some projects don't pan out, this policy has led to groundbreaking innovations like Gmail and Google Maps. The takeaway? If employees are too afraid to fail, they'll never innovate. A safe space for failure invites risk-taking, which fuels creativity and progress.

Turning Mistakes into Learning Opportunities

Supervisors who frame failures as learning experiences rather than setbacks create an environment of continuous improvement. For example, when a marketing campaign underperforms, an empathetic leader doesn't place blame but instead gathers the team for a postmortem discussion. Together, they examine what went wrong, what could have been done differently, and how similar mistakes can be avoided in the future. This approach shifts failure from something to be feared into a tool for refinement and progress. Failure isn't the end—it's a step forward. Leaders who treat failure as feedback rather than finality cultivate a team that learns, adapts, and ultimately thrives.

Balancing Accountability with Support

Creating a space for failure doesn't mean there are no consequences. It means there is a balance between accountability and support.

- **Accountability:** Employees must understand that while mistakes are acceptable, they must also learn from them.
- **Support:** Supervisors provide guidance and resources to help employees improve and succeed.

Case Study: TechCo's Software Development Team

TechCo is a software company working on a groundbreaking app. Alex, a new supervisor, is leading a team of experienced developers and new hires. The stakes are high and deadlines are tight.

Step 1: Establish a Culture of Empathy

- Action: Alex holds a team meeting to invite feedback on deadlines. He actively listens, encouraging employees to voice concerns.
- Outcome: Developers feel heard and appreciated. Their input leads to a decision to adjust the project timeline, which improves morale and prevents burnout.

Step 2: Create a Safe Space for Failure

- Action: Alex adopts a "fail fast, learn fast" approach. Team members are encouraged to try experimental solutions, knowing mistakes are part of learning.
- Outcome: One developer tests a new app feature that initially crashes, but after reflection, the team develops a better approach.

Step 3: Balance Accountability with Support

- Action: A critical bug crashes the app before a client demo. Instead of assigning blame, Alex gathers the team to analyze what went wrong.
- Outcome: The team identifies the root cause, resolves it, and strengthens internal testing protocols. This experience reinforces a "fix it, don't fear it" culture.

Step 4: Provide Constructive Feedback

- Action: Alex holds one-on-one meetings to discuss the bug incident, focusing on strengths, growth areas, and lessons learned.

- Outcome: Employees feel valued and supported, with one developer saying, "I appreciate that Alex saw this as a learning opportunity, not a failure."

Step 5: Foster a Growth Mindset

- Action: Alex emphasizes continuous learning, sharing resources, and encouraging employees to experiment with new skills.
- Outcome: Employees become more engaged, curious, and willing to explore new ideas.

Key Takeaways

1. Empathy fosters engagement: Empathy builds trust, encourages honest dialogue, and creates emotional connections that inspire employee loyalty.
2. Safe spaces lead to innovation: Employees who feel safe making mistakes take creative risks, leading to breakthrough ideas.
3. Accountability and support are not opposites: Balancing accountability with support ensures employees grow from their mistakes, not fear them.
4. Learning happens in discomfort: Growth happens outside of comfort zones. If employees are too comfortable, they aren't growing.
5. Feedback fuels growth: Use mistakes as teaching moments, not as opportunities to assign blame.

Conclusion: Leading with Empathy, Learning from Failure

Supervisors often feel pressure to appear "perfect" in front of their teams. But great leaders don't strive for perfection—they strive for progress. Empathy and failure are not signs of weakness but proof of wisdom and adaptability.

An empathetic leader creates trust, reduces fear, and opens lines of communication. A leader who allows space for failure encourages creativity, learning, and innovation. When you combine these qualities, you create a team that isn't afraid to take risks, offer bold ideas, and face challenges head-on.

Mistakes are inevitable. What matters is how you respond. Will you blame? Or will you build?

The most effective leaders understand that true leadership isn't about projecting perfection—it's about fostering growth. Research underscores the value of empathy in leadership. McKinsey & Company highlights that empathetic leadership enhances workplace culture and organizational health, leading to improved productivity and stronger team dynamics (McKinsey & Company 2024).

Furthermore, embracing a learning-oriented approach to failure is crucial. Harvard Business Review emphasizes that distinguishing between productive failures (those arising from thoughtful experimentation) and avoidable mistakes is essential. Creating an environment that encourages smart risk-taking and views failure as a pathway to growth fosters psychological safety and continuous improvement (HBR 2023).

Empathy strengthens trust, communication, and collaboration, creating an environment where employees feel heard and valued. When employees know their leaders genuinely care, they are more likely to contribute ideas, take initiative, and remain committed to the team's success. Likewise, creating a safe space for failure fosters innovation and continuous learning. Supervisors who shift the perception of failure from something to be feared into a valuable learning opportunity encourage problem solving, risk-taking, and long-term growth.

Great supervisors don't prevent failure—they guide their teams through it. By reframing mistakes as learning experiences and modeling resilience, leaders cultivate a team that thrives in the face of challenges. Instead of asking, *"Who is responsible?"* they ask, *"What can we learn?"* and *"How can we improve?"* This shift in mindset transforms failure from a setback into a steppingstone for growth.

Your effectiveness as a leader isn't measured by how many mistakes your team avoids but by how well they learn, adapt, and grow from their experiences. By embracing empathetic leadership and fostering a failure-friendly culture, you will build a high-performing team that is not only capable but also confident in pushing boundaries, taking risks, and driving meaningful success. Failure isn't final—it's feedback. And when you lead with that perspective, your team will rise to meet every challenge with courage and resilience.

Your role as a leader is not to eliminate mistakes but to create an environment where employees can learn, adapt, and thrive in the face of challenges. By leading with empathy and allowing space to fail, you will cultivate a team that is resilient, engaged, and equipped to meet future challenges with confidence.

CHAPTER 12

Becoming a Continuous Learner: Supervisor for Life

Lifelong learning is like upgrading your phone. It's annoying, it's costly, and you're pretty sure the new version will have bugs, but you'll be a lot better off in the long run.

Becoming a supervisor marks the beginning of an ongoing journey of growth and development. While mastering the fundamentals of leadership is crucial, the reality is that supervision is an ever-evolving role. What works today may not work tomorrow, and staying stagnant means falling behind. The landscape of supervision is ever-changing, requiring continual adaptation to new challenges and changing team dynamics. Lifelong learning emerges not merely as an asset but as a necessity for sustained success in leadership roles.

This chapter explores what it means to become a "Supervisor for Life," focusing on the mindset and habits required for continuous learning. It emphasizes the importance of growth, adaptability, and a commitment to learning from everyone and every experience. By the end of this chapter, you'll have a blueprint for how to keep growing, even after you've "mastered" the basics of supervision.

Embracing a Growth Mindset

What is a Growth Mindset?

A growth mindset, a concept developed by psychologist Carol Dweck, is the belief that abilities, intelligence, and leadership capacity are not fixed but can be developed with effort, learning, and persistence. For supervisors, this means that mistakes are not failures but learning opportunities.

Supervisors with a growth mindset are more adaptable, open to feedback, and willing to embrace new challenges. They recognize that their role will evolve, and they accept this reality instead of fighting against it.

As a supervisor, your success hinges on your ability to shift from "I already know this" to "What can I learn from this?"

Adapting to New Challenges

Supervision isn't a checklist you complete—it's a dynamic role that requires constant adaptation. Whether it's managing remote teams, responding to organizational change, or adopting new technologies, supervisors who embrace change rather than resist it have a distinct advantage.

Example: When telehealth technology was introduced in the health care sector, many supervisors resisted the shift. However, those who embraced it by learning the technology and encouraging their teams to do the same found that their departments operated more efficiently and with higher patient satisfaction.

Takeaway: Supervisors who view change as an opportunity to grow, rather than a threat to overcome, are the ones who thrive.

Case Study: Sarah's Journey

When Sarah was promoted to supervisor at a marketing agency, she was overwhelmed. She feared her lack of experience would make her a target for criticism. After attending a workshop on growth mindset, she began to reframe her thinking. Instead of seeing her inexperience as a liability, she viewed it as a chance to learn. She asked questions, sought feedback, and grew into the role. Today, she's regarded as one of the most adaptable leaders in her organization.

Lesson learned: Your experience level does not define your potential as a supervisor—your mindset does.

Continuous Skill Building

Why It Matters

The shelf life of skills is shorter than ever. What you know today could be obsolete tomorrow. Supervisors who are proactive in upgrading their skills stay relevant, respected, and ready to lead their teams into the future.

Example: Consider a supervisor at a manufacturing company. Ten years ago, managing production schedules and inventory tracking was done on spreadsheets. Today, it's done with predictive analytics and AI-driven software. The supervisor who stays ahead of this curve by learning new tools remains indispensable.

How to Stay Sharp

- Formal education: Take advantage of workshops, online courses, and certifications.
- Microlearning: Consume short, focused lessons on relevant topics (e.g., LinkedIn Learning, TED Talks).
- Peer learning: Build a community of fellow supervisors who share their best practices.
- Shadowing: Observe more experienced supervisors, asking questions, and studying their habits.

Set a quarterly learning goal, like mastering one new tool, reading a book on leadership, or attending a workshop.

Curiosity and Open-Mindedness

The Power of Curiosity

Curiosity is the spark that drives continuous learning. Without it, supervisors operate on autopilot, following routines instead of seeking better ways to lead. By asking "Why?" and "What if?" supervisors can challenge assumptions, uncover new perspectives, and discover more effective strategies.

Learning from Your Team

Your team is one of the richest sources of knowledge you have. Every team member brings unique skills, perspectives, and experiences. Supervisors who actively seek to learn from their teams are better equipped to solve problems and make informed decisions.

Example: A customer service supervisor might hold monthly "Team Wisdom" sessions where employees are invited to share lessons learned from their toughest calls. These insights not only improve service but also build team cohesion.

Learning from Peers

Why reinvent the wheel when other supervisors have already figured it out? Join supervisor networks, attend industry events, and participate in mentorship programs. Learning from your peers can accelerate your growth while exposing you to fresh ideas.

If your company doesn't offer a mentorship program, create one. Connect with supervisors in different departments to exchange insights.

Exploring New Experiences

Growth doesn't happen in comfort zones. Supervisors should seek out new projects and experiences to broaden their leadership skills. Volunteer for cross-functional teams, temporary assignments, or initiatives outside your department.

Example: A finance supervisor volunteers to lead an employee wellness initiative for their company. In doing so, they learn new skills in team engagement and cultural awareness, which later benefit their leadership style.

Historical Example: IBM's Reinvention Under Lou Gerstner

In the early 1990s, IBM was in crisis. It was losing money, market share, and relevance. Enter Lou Gerstner, who transformed IBM by adopting a continuous learning philosophy for himself and the organization.

Key Takeaways from Gerstner's Leadership

- Growth mindset: He saw change as essential, not optional.
- Employee feedback: He met with employees at all levels to gain insights into the company's real challenges.
- Skill building: He invested in employee development, upskilling the workforce to align with the company's new direction.
- Agility: He shifted IBM from a hardware company to a services company, anticipating market trends.

Lesson Learned: If IBM—a 100-year-old giant—can reinvent itself, so can you. Stay curious, stay humble, and stay committed to learning.

Fictional Scenario: Alex, the New Tech Supervisor

Alex, a newly promoted supervisor at Tech Innovations, was thrown into the fire. His team faced aggressive deadlines and shifting client requirements. Here's how he mastered continuous learning on the job:

1. Growth mindset: Instead of complaining about tight deadlines, Alex studied agile project management.
2. Continuous learning: He signed his team up for online coding bootcamps to upskill them for future projects.
3. Peer learning: Alex regularly met with other supervisors to share project management best practices.
4. Exploring new tools: He implemented a project management tool that streamlined workflows and improved efficiency.

Result: Alex's team became more efficient, reduced errors, and delivered projects on time.

Conclusion: The Supervisor's Learning Loop

Becoming a supervisor is not the end of your learning journey—it's the beginning of a lifelong commitment to growth. The best supervisors understand that leadership is not about having all the answers but about continuously seeking better questions. Success in supervision comes from staying adaptable, embracing new challenges, and maintaining a mindset of curiosity and development.

Three Key Takeaways:

1. Never stop learning—The workplace is constantly evolving, and so must you. The skills that made you successful today may not be enough for tomorrow. Stay curious, seek knowledge, and commit to lifelong learning.
2. Mistakes are lessons—Every challenge and setback is an opportunity to refine your approach. The best supervisors treat mistakes as steppingstones toward mastery, learning from each experience to become stronger leaders.
3. Lead by example—If you want a team that is engaged, growing, and high-performing, you must model those behaviors yourself. Demonstrate a commitment to learning, personal development, and adaptability in everything you do.

As you move forward in your supervisory journey, remember that leadership is not a static role—it is a continuous evolution. The strongest leaders are those who remain open to new ideas, challenge their own assumptions, and embrace growth as an ongoing process. By committing to continuous learning, you not only become a better supervisor but also a more resilient, insightful, and inspiring leader.

The future belongs to those who never stop learning. Embrace that journey, and you will not only shape the success of your team but also define your own legacy as a leader.

Conclusion:
Your Supervisory Journey
Begins Here

Congratulations on reaching the final pages of *Leading From Day One*. But before you close this book, take a moment to reflect. You've just equipped yourself with the tools, techniques, and mindset shifts that separate good supervisors from great ones. More importantly, you've taken the first step on a journey that never truly ends—because great supervisors never stop learning, growing, and leading.

If there's one truth to remember as you step into (or continue) your supervisory role, it's this: ***Leadership is not about being perfect—it's about being present***. It's about showing up every day with a commitment to growth—for yourself and your team. You don't need to have all the answers, but you do need to be willing to ask questions, listen intently, and guide your team toward solutions.

This journey isn't always easy. You'll face doubt, missteps, and moments where you question your own abilities. And that's okay. Every supervisor who has ever succeeded has felt that same weight of responsibility. But here's the secret: *You're not supposed to do it alone.* Leadership isn't about carrying the burden yourself—it's about sharing it with your team, building trust, and encouraging everyone to pull together toward shared goals.

Throughout these chapters, we've explored the essential building blocks of effective supervision:

- From "Doer" to leader: Letting go of your old role and stepping fully into a leadership mindset
- Building trust and rapport: Creating the psychological safety that fuels high-performing teams
- Setting expectations and feedback: Mastering clarity and accountability, the twin engines of team success

- Managing time and priorities: Leading with focus, not frenzy
- Delegating with purpose: Letting go, so others can rise up
- Handling conflict with empathy: Navigating tough conversations with courage, not avoidance
- Driving growth and development: Coaching your team to their highest potential
- Leading through change: Being the calm in the storm of uncertainty
- Hiring with intent: Building a team that works for today and grows for tomorrow
- Performance management and accountability: Turning annual reviews into continuous growth conversations
- Empathy and space to fail: Recognizing that mistakes are not failures, but the beginning of breakthroughs
- Becoming a lifelong learner: Embracing the endless journey of leadership development

These principles aren't just skills to check off a list. They're the foundation of something far greater—your legacy. Because make no mistake, *you are building a legacy*. Every person you support, every team member you coach, every challenge you overcome leaves an indelible mark. Your success as a supervisor isn't measured by your individual achievements; it's measured by the people you empower to succeed.

You Are Ready

So, what now? You've read the stories, explored the strategies, and even reflected on your own growth as a leader. But theory alone doesn't make you a leader. *Action does.*

Here's where I challenge you: Don't let this book sit on your shelf as a "nice read." Instead, treat it like a guide, a reference, a playbook you return to when you face a new challenge. The worksheets aren't just "extras"—they are your tools for reflection, action, and growth. Use them. Revise them. Own them.

As you move forward, keep this in mind: *You will make mistakes. You will question yourself. You will doubt your ability to lead.* But every mistake is a lesson in disguise. The only true mistake is the one you fail to learn from.

When you face moments of uncertainty (and you will), ask yourself these questions:

- Am I focused on outcomes or output?
- Am I leading with trust, or am I leading with control?
- Am I creating clarity for my team, or am I contributing to confusion?
- Am I empowering my team to grow, or am I trying to do it all myself?

This Is Not Goodbye

This is not the end of the playbook—it's the beginning of your leadership journey. You've learned how to navigate uncertainty, master delegation, and develop the confidence to lead with empathy. You are prepared. Will you feel fully ready on Day 1? Maybe not. But guess what? *Nobody does.* The best supervisors learn as they lead.

You now have a framework, a set of principles, and a playbook that will support you through every twist and turn. If you get stuck, revisit a chapter. If you need a reminder, return to the worksheets. And if you ever feel like you're not ready, remember this: *You already are.* If you've read this far, if you've reflected on your growth, if you're committed to your team's success—you are ready.

Leadership is not about perfection, it's about progress. It's about learning, unlearning, and relearning as you go. Your first 90 days as a supervisor will be formative, but they won't define you. It's the days, months, and years that follow that shape your legacy.

A Final Thought

If I could travel back in time and hand this book to my younger self, I would. It would have saved me from my early mistakes, like that cringe-worthy moment of "taking over" my team's project instead of trusting them to succeed. I'd tell my younger self, *"Trust them. They're more ready than you think."*

But I can't go back in time. Neither can you. What we can do is move forward—better, wiser, and stronger than before. I hope this playbook serves as the roadmap I never had. A guide to help you avoid the mistakes I made, embrace the lessons I learned, and become the kind of supervisor your team will be proud to follow.

Your journey is just beginning. Step forward with confidence. Lead with empathy. Take action with clarity. Be patient with yourself, and never stop growing.

Your team is waiting. They're ready for a leader. They're ready for you.

Worksheets

Chapter 1: Transitioning to a Supervisory Role

Worksheet 1: Understanding Your Transition

This worksheet will help you reflect on the changes you're experiencing and identify how to approach your new role effectively.

1. **Defining Your Shift**
   A. **What is the biggest difference between your previous role and your new supervisory role?**

   _____

   _____

   B. **What excites you most about becoming a supervisor?**

   _____

   _____

   C. **What concerns do you have about this transition?**

   _____

   _____

2. **Letting Go of Your Old Role**
   New supervisors often struggle with stepping away from the daily tasks they used to handle. Reflect on the following:
   A. **List three tasks you used to take pride in as an individual contributor:**
      1. _____
      2. _____
      3. _____
   B. **How might holding onto these tasks prevent you from being an effective leader?**

   _____

   _____

C. **What are three new responsibilities you must focus on as a supervisor?**

1. _____

2. _____

3. _____

Worksheet 2: Shifting from Peer to Leader

Managing former colleagues can be one of the most complex aspects of becoming a supervisor. Use this worksheet to plan your transition.

1. **Understanding the Change in Relationships**
   A. **How do you anticipate your relationships with former peers will change?**

   _____

   _____

   B. **What challenges might arise when managing former peers?**
      ☐ Navigating personal friendships while maintaining authority
      ☐ Handling potential resentment or skepticism about my promotion
      ☐ Setting new expectations without damaging relationships
      ☐ Addressing conflicts that arise from shifting dynamics
      ☐ Other: _____

2. **Setting the Right Tone as a Leader**
   A. **What are three ways you can communicate your leadership role to your team while maintaining trust and respect?**
      1. _____
      2. _____
      3. _____

   B. **How will you handle situations where former peers test your authority or challenge your decisions?**

   _____

   _____

Worksheet 3: Identity Shift—From Doer to Leader

Your new role isn't just about responsibilities—it's about adopting a leadership identity.

1. **Your Leadership Mindset**
   A. **How would you define your personal leadership philosophy?**

   _____

   _____

   B. **Which of the following mindset shifts do you need to make?**
      (Check all that apply.)
      ☐ I define success based on my team's achievements, not just my own.
      ☐ I must shift from "doing" tasks to **guiding and enabling** my team.
      ☐ I need to make decisions based on **team success** rather than personal efficiency.
      ☐ My priority is developing my team rather than proving my own expertise.
      ☐ Leadership is about **building relationships and trust**, not just giving orders.

2. **Mapping Your Leadership Growth**
   Think about **where you are now** and **where you want to be** in the coming months.

Leadership Skill	Current Confidence Level (1–5)	Goal in 3 Months (1–5)
Managing former peers	_____	_____
Setting expectations	_____	_____
Balancing strategic and operational thinking	_____	_____
Handling difficult conversations	_____	_____
Building credibility as a leader	_____	_____

C. What's one action you can take this week to start building leadership confidence?

_____

_____

Checklists

Checklist 1: Key Supervisor Mindset Shifts

Use this checklist to ensure you're making the necessary shifts as you transition into leadership.

✓ **I recognize that my success is based on my team's success, not just my personal achievements.**
✓ **I understand that my primary role is to enable, guide, and support my team, rather than handling all tasks myself.**
✓ **I have started adjusting my communication approach to reflect my leadership role.**
✓ **I am prepared for potential challenges in managing former peers and have strategies to address them.**
✓ **I am beginning to shift my focus from operational work to broader team and strategic priorities.**

Reflection Questions

Take time to reflect on your leadership transition and consider how you want to grow in this role.

1. **What has been the most challenging part of transitioning into leadership so far?**

   _____

   _____

2. **What is one skill or mindset shift you will focus on developing in the next 30 days?**

   _____

   _____

3. **What do you want your team to say about you as a leader 6 months from now? What steps will you take to make that vision a reality?**

   _____

   _____

Worksheet: Developing Your 90-Day Supervisor Plan

A strong first 90 days set the foundation for long-term success in your supervisory role. Use this structured plan to **clarify your goals, establish credibility, and begin making an impact**.

Step 1: Setting Your Leadership Priorities

Before diving into the details of your first 90 days, take a moment to reflect on what you want to achieve in this period.

A. Your Vision for Your First 90 Days
1. What are the top **three goals** you want to accomplish as a new supervisor?
    - _____
    - _____
    - _____
2. What **challenges or concerns** do you anticipate, and how will you address them?
    - _____
    - _____

Step 2: The 90-Day Leadership Roadmap

Use this framework to break down your first 3 months into **focused, manageable phases**.

Phase 1: First 30 Days—Learn & Listen

Your primary goal in this phase is to **observe, listen, and build relationships** with your team and key stakeholders.

☐ **Conduct One-on-One Meetings:** Meet with each team member to understand their roles, challenges, and career aspirations. Ask:
- "What do you enjoy most about your job?"
- "What challenges are you currently facing?"
- "How can I best support you?"

☐ **Understand Team Dynamics:**
  • Identify key influencers within the team.
  • Recognize existing workflows and challenges.
  • Observe how decisions are made.

☐ **Clarify Expectations with Your Manager:**
  • Understand leadership's priorities for your role.
  • Define success metrics for your first 6 months.

☐ **Assess Workflows & Priorities:**
  • Review ongoing projects and team responsibilities.
  • Identify any bottlenecks or inefficiencies.

☐ **Personal Leadership Reflection:**
  • What surprised you about your new role?
  • What early insights do you have about your team's strengths and needs?

Phase 2: Days 31 to 60—Establish and Communicate Expectations

In this phase, focus on **establishing credibility, clarifying expectations, and identifying quick wins**.

☐ **Clarify Team Roles and Responsibilities:**
  • Ensure everyone understands their responsibilities.
  • Identify areas where clarity or restructuring is needed.

☐ **Set Short-Term Performance Goals:**
  • Define clear, achievable objectives for the team.
  • Align team efforts with broader organizational goals.

☐ **Identify and Implement Quick Wins:**
  • Find small but meaningful improvements that boost morale and efficiency.
  • Address "low-hanging fruit" issues that have been overlooked.

☐ **Begin Adjusting Leadership Approach as Needed:**
  • Reflect on how your leadership style is received by the team.
  • Make adjustments based on feedback and team needs.

☐ **Check In with Your Manager:**
- Discuss your observations and progress.
- Confirm that your leadership priorities align with company expectations.

Phase 3: Days 61 to 90—Take Ownership and Drive Progress

Now, your focus shifts to **reinforcing new expectations, improving team performance, and shaping a long-term vision**.

☐ **Reinforce Team Culture and Accountability:**
- Hold team members accountable for commitments.
- Continue fostering open communication.

☐ **Address Deeper Challenges:**
- Start tackling more complex or systemic issues.
- Ensure team members have the support and tools they need.

☐ **Develop a Long-Term Leadership Plan:**
- Outline personal leadership goals for the next 6 to 12 months.
- Identify key development opportunities for the team.

☐ **Conduct a 90-Day Review:**
- Reflect on what went well and what needs improvement.
- Ask for feedback from team members and leadership.
- Adjust strategies based on lessons learned.

Step 3: Personal Leadership Check-In

At the end of your 90-day period, reflect on your progress and areas for continued growth.

1. What are the **three biggest lessons** you've learned in your first 90 days?
   - _____
   - _____
   - _____

2. What leadership habits have been most effective for you?

    o _____

3. What adjustments will you make moving forward?

    o _____

Final Checklist: Have You Successfully Completed Your 90-Day Plan?

✓ I have built strong relationships with my team through one-on-one meetings.

✓ I understand my team's challenges, workflows, and performance expectations.

✓ I have aligned my leadership approach with organizational goals.

✓ I have set clear expectations and identified areas for improvement.

✓ I have started implementing small but impactful improvements.

✓ I am comfortable making leadership decisions and guiding my team.

✓ I have reflected on my leadership growth and identified next steps.

Closing Thought

The **first 90 days** lay the foundation for long-term success as a supervisor. **Take time to reflect on your progress, learn from your experiences, and commit to continuous growth.** Each new challenge is an opportunity to develop your leadership style and make a meaningful impact on your team.

Chapter 2: Building Trust and Rapport with Your Team

As a new supervisor, trust is your most valuable asset. This worksheet will help you reflect on your current approach to trust-building, develop strategies for fostering trust within your team, and track your progress over time.

Section 1: Assessing Your Current Trust-Building Approach

Before implementing new strategies, take a moment to evaluate where you stand.

1. **Rate Yourself (1–5) on the Following Trust-Building Behaviors:**
   (1 = Rarely, 5 = Always)
   - I follow through on my commitments. _____
   - I communicate openly and transparently with my team. _____
   - I acknowledge and validate team members' emotions. _____
   - I create a safe space for questions and concerns. _____
   - I regularly check in with my team members to understand their needs. _____
   - I admit when I don't have the answers and seek input. _____
   - I provide recognition and credit for my team's contributions. _____

2. **What specific behaviors have helped you build trust in past roles?**
   - _____
   - _____

3. **What is one area where you'd like to improve your ability to build trust?**
   - _____
   - _____

Section 2: Establishing Trust in Your First 90 Days

Use this structured **90-day roadmap** to intentionally build trust within your team.

Phase 1: First 30 Days—Establish a Foundation of Reliability

☐ **Hold Individual Meetings**
  - Learn about each team member's work style, challenges, and goals.
  - Ask: "What can I do to support you in your role?"

☐ **Demonstrate Follow-Through**
  - Keep your commitments, no matter how small.
  - Respond to e-mails and messages in a timely manner.

☐ **Communicate Early and Often**
  - Keep your team informed about key decisions and changes.
  - Avoid surprises—share the reasoning behind your decisions.

☐ **Be Visible and Approachable**
  - Make time for informal check-ins.
  - Show genuine interest in your team's success and well-being.

Phase 2: Days 31 to 60—Strengthen Team Dynamics

☐ **Host Transparent Team Meetings**
  - Clearly communicate expectations and decision-making processes.
  - Encourage open dialogue and input from team members.

☐ **Give Credit Publicly, Address Issues Privately**
  - Recognize contributions in team settings.
  - Handle performance concerns in one-on-one discussions.

☐ **Demonstrate Professional Vulnerability**
  - Share what you're learning in your new role.
  - Seek feedback on your leadership approach.

☐ **Begin Establishing Psychological Safety**
- Respond constructively to mistakes and learning opportunities.
- Reinforce that all ideas and perspectives are welcome.

Phase 3: Days 61 to 90—Reinforce Trust Through Actions

☐ **Deliver on Early Promises**
- Review commitments made in your first 30 days and ensure follow-through.
- Revisit concerns raised by team members and provide updates.

☐ **Continue to Actively Listen**
- Hold check-ins to ask, "What's working? What needs adjustment?"
- Practice the **HEAR Method**:
  - **Hold space** for concerns.
  - **Engage** with thoughtful questions.
  - **Acknowledge** emotions.
  - **Reflect** key points back for understanding.

☐ **Develop Individual Growth Plans**
- Show commitment to team members' development.
- Provide opportunities for professional growth and learning.

☐ **Encourage Constructive Risk-Taking**
- Reinforce that reasonable mistakes are learning opportunities.
- Support team members in problem solving rather than punishing failure.

Section 3: Handling Trust-Breaking Situations

Trust is fragile and can be easily damaged by miscommunication or inconsistent actions. Use this section to anticipate and plan for difficult situations.

Scenario-Based Reflection

1. **A team member expresses concern that you are favoring one person over others.**
   - How would you handle this perception?
   - _____
   - _____

2. **You made a mistake in a decision that impacted the team.**
   - How will you address this openly while maintaining credibility?
   - _____
   - _____

3. **Your team is reluctant to share feedback with you.**
   - What steps can you take to create a more open environment?
   - _____
   - _____

Checklist: Are You Building Trust Effectively?

✓ I actively listen and engage with my team members.
✓ I communicate openly and share the reasoning behind my decisions.
✓ I follow through on commitments and deliver on promises.
✓ I encourage open dialogue and create psychological safety.
✓ I give credit where it's due and recognize contributions.
✓ I provide constructive feedback while supporting individual growth.
✓ I model vulnerability by admitting mistakes and seeking feedback.

Reflection: Commit to Trust-Building in Your Leadership

Trust is not built overnight—it requires **consistent, intentional actions**. Use this final reflection to set trust-building goals for the months ahead.

1. **What is one behavior you will commit to improving in your leadership approach?**
   o _____

2. **How will you measure whether trust is growing within your team?**
   o _____

3. **What are three specific actions you will take in the next 30 days to strengthen trust?**
   o _____
   o _____
   o _____

Closing Thought

Trust is the foundation of leadership. When you prioritize transparency, reliability, and active listening, you create a team culture that thrives on collaboration, innovation, and mutual respect. Keep investing in trust—it's the most valuable leadership currency you have

Chapter 3: Setting Clear Expectations and Providing Feedback

Worksheet 1: Establishing Clear Expectations

Objective:

Define and refine expectations at the foundational, performance, and growth levels to ensure clarity and alignment.

Step 1: Defining Expectations

For each level of expectation, write down specific expectations for your team members.

Expectation level	Description	Example
Foundational Expectations	Define core job responsibilities, professional conduct, and quality standards.	"Respond to all customer inquiries within 24 hours."
Performance Goals	Set measurable targets tied to individual and team success.	"Increase sales by 10% over the next quarter through targeted outreach."
Growth Expectations	Encourage professional development and skill building.	"Complete a leadership training course within six months."

Step 2: Communicating Expectations Clearly

1. How will you communicate these expectations to your team?
2. What methods will you use to reinforce them (e.g., team meetings, one-on-one discussions, written guidelines)?
3. How will you ensure your team understands and commits to these expectations?

Step 3: Checking for Alignment

- Do these expectations align with team and company goals?
- Have you set both immediate and long-term goals?
- Are these expectations realistic and achievable?

Worksheet 2: Setting SMART Goals

Objective:

Develop well-defined goals using the **SMART** framework.

SMART Goal Breakdown

Use the table below to transform a broad goal into a SMART goal.

SMART criteria	Your goal	Example
Specific	Define what exactly needs to be achieved.	"Increase customer retention." → "Reduce customer churn by 20% through improved onboarding."
Measurable	Establish quantifiable metrics.	"Customer satisfaction scores will increase from 85% to 90% in six months."
Achievable	Ensure the goal is realistic given time and resources.	"Based on past trends, a 5% quarterly improvement is reasonable."
Relevant	Align with company objectives.	"Customer retention contributes to long-term profitability."
Time-bound	Set deadlines and milestones.	"Achieve this within Q2."

Final SMART Goal:

Rewrite your goal using the SMART framework.

Worksheet 3: Structuring Effective Feedback

Objective:

Use the **Situation–Behavior–Impact (SBI) Model** to provide clear, actionable feedback.

Step 1: Identifying a Feedback Scenario

Think of a recent situation where you need to provide feedback (positive or constructive). Describe it briefly below.

Example Scenario:

A team member repeatedly missed project deadlines, impacting team workflow.

Step 2: Applying the SBI Model

Complete the following table based on your scenario.

SBI step	Your response	Example
Situation	Identify when and where the event occurred.	"During last week's team meeting…"
Behavior	Describe what the employee did (focus on observable actions, not assumptions).	"You didn't submit your portion of the project by the agreed deadline."
Impact	Explain how the behavior affected the team, project, or organization.	"This delayed the project timeline and caused others to work overtime."

Step 3: Delivering the Feedback

1. How will you approach the conversation to keep it constructive?
2. What action steps or support will you provide to help the employee improve?

Checklist 1: Avoiding Common Feedback Pitfalls

Before delivering feedback, review this checklist to ensure effectiveness.

- ✓ **Avoid the Feedback Sandwich**—Be direct and separate praise from areas for improvement.
- ✓ **Be Specific**—Use concrete examples instead of vague statements.
- ✓ **Encourage Two-Way Dialogue**—Allow employees to share their perspective.
- ✓ **Offer Actionable Steps**—Provide clear suggestions for improvement.
- ✓ **Follow Up**—Check in later to assess progress.

Checklist 2: Managing Difficult Feedback Conversations

Use this checklist to ensure you're prepared for a tough feedback discussion.

Preparation

- ✓ Gather specific examples and data.
- ✓ Plan key points you want to cover.
- ✓ Choose an appropriate time and private setting.

Delivery

- ✓ Stick to observable behaviors, not personal judgments.
- ✓ Keep the conversation fact-based and professional.
- ✓ Maintain a calm and composed tone.
- ✓ Encourage the employee to share their thoughts.

Follow-Up

- ✓ Summarize key takeaways from the discussion.
- ✓ Develop a plan for improvement with measurable milestones.
- ✓ Schedule follow-ups to check progress.

Checklist 3: Reinforcing Expectations and Feedback Over Time

To ensure long-term effectiveness, supervisors must consistently reinforce expectations and feedback.

Weekly Actions

✓ Check in with employees to assess progress on expectations.
✓ Recognize achievements and provide timely praise.
✓ Identify any gaps in understanding or execution of expectations.

Monthly Actions

✓ Hold one-on-one meetings to review progress on performance goals.
✓ Offer structured feedback using the SBI model.
✓ Adjust goals as needed based on workload and team needs.

Quarterly Actions

✓ Reevaluate expectations and ensure alignment with company objectives.
✓ Collect feedback from team members on clarity of expectations.
✓ Celebrate wins and analyze challenges from the past quarter.

These worksheets and checklists will help you set clear expectations, create SMART goals, and provide effective feedback using structured methods.

Chapter 4: Managing Time and Priorities

Worksheet 1: Analyzing Your Time Management Habits

Objective:

Identify how you currently spend your time and recognize areas for improvement.

Step 1: Track Your Time

For the next **three days**, record your activities in 30-minute increments. Categorize each task into one of the four **Eisenhower Matrix quadrants**:

Time slot	Activity	Quadrant (I, II, III, IV)	Comments
8:00–8:30 a.m.	Responding to e-mails	III	Some e-mails were urgent, but most could have waited.
8:30–9:00 a.m.	Preparing for a team meeting	II	Good use of time for strategic planning.

Step 2: Reflection Questions

1. Which quadrant are most of your tasks falling into?
2. What tasks should you be focusing on more?
3. Where are you spending time on non-essential activities?
4. What tasks can be scheduled, delegated, or eliminated?

Worksheet 2: Applying the Eisenhower Matrix

Objective:

Categorize your current tasks using the Eisenhower Matrix and develop a prioritization strategy.

Step 1: Identify Your Current Tasks

List 10 tasks from your workload and place them in the correct quadrant.

Task	Urgent & important (I)	Important but not urgent (II)	Urgent but not important (III)	Neither urgent nor important (IV)
Example Task	Fixing a major client issue	Developing a long-term strategy	Answering routine e-mails	Scrolling through social media

Step 2: Strategy for Each Quadrant

- **Quadrant I (Urgent and Important)**—Plan time to address these immediately, but consider how to prevent them in the future.
- **Quadrant II (Important but Not Urgent)**—Schedule dedicated time to work on these high-impact tasks.
- **Quadrant III (Urgent but Not Important)**—Delegate or automate these whenever possible.
- **Quadrant IV (Neither Urgent nor Important)**—Eliminate or minimize these activities.

Action Step:

1. Choose three quadrant II tasks and schedule time for them in the next 2 weeks.
2. Identify at least two quadrant III tasks that can be delegated.
3. Select one quadrant IV activity to eliminate immediately.

Worksheet 3: Time Blocking for Supervisors

Objective:

Use **time blocking** to ensure focus on high-priority tasks.

Step 1: Define Your Ideal Weekly Schedule

Block out time in your calendar for key supervisory activities.

Time block	Activity	Category (Quadrant I, II, III, IV)
8:00–9:30 a.m.	Strategic planning and team development	II
10:00–11:00 a.m.	One-on-one meetings with team	II
11:00–12:00 p.m.	Handling urgent team issues	I
2:00–3:00 p.m.	e-mail and administrative tasks	III

Step 2: Reflection Questions

1. Are you dedicating enough time to **quadrant II** activities?
2. Which time slots are consistently taken up by unplanned urgent tasks?
3. What adjustments can you make to protect your most valuable time?

Worksheet 4: Reducing Time-Wasters

Objective:

Identify and eliminate low-value tasks.

Step 1: Identify Common Time-Wasters

Check any activities that apply to your work routine.

- ✓ Attending meetings without a clear agenda.
- ✓ Checking e-mails multiple times per hour.
- ✓ Answering non-urgent requests immediately.
- ✓ Spending excessive time on perfectionist tendencies.
- ✓ Allowing unplanned interruptions to dictate your schedule.

Step 2: Eliminating or Controlling Time-Wasters For each checked item, write one action step to reduce or eliminate the time-wasting behavior.

Time-waster	Strategy to reduce it
Checking e-mails too frequently	Schedule set times for e-mail review (e.g., 10 a.m. and 3 p.m.).
Unnecessary meetings	Require agendas and decline non-essential meetings.
Immediate response to every message	Set "office hours" for questions instead of constant availability.

Checklist 1: Time Management for Supervisors

✓ Start each day with **a prioritized task list.**

✓ Use the **Eisenhower Matrix** to categorize tasks before acting on them.

✓ Protect at least **40 percent of your time for strategic thinking and team development.**

✓ **Time block** your schedule to prevent constant disruptions.

✓ Identify **low-priority tasks** and delegate them where possible.

✓ Reduce **quadrant IV (time-wasting) activities** to increase focus.

✓ Schedule **weekly reflections** to evaluate and adjust your time management strategy.

Checklist 2: Leading a Productive Team

✓ Hold a **weekly prioritization meeting** to align tasks with team objectives.

✓ Communicate clearly about which tasks are **urgent vs. important.**

✓ Encourage team members to **track and analyze their time** for efficiency.

✓ Delegate effectively to **reduce supervisor overload** and **develop team skills.**

✓ Monitor and adjust team workflow **to prevent burnout.**

Checklist 3: Managing Interruptions and Urgent Requests

✓ **Ask if the task is truly urgent** or if it can wait.

✓ If the task is **quadrant III (Urgent but Not Important)** → **Delegate it.**

✓ If the task is **quadrant II (Important but Not Urgent)** → **Schedule it.**

✓ If the task is **quadrant IV (Neither Urgent nor Important)** → **Eliminate it.**

✓ Set boundaries to protect focused work time (e.g., **silent work hours** or **no-meeting blocks**).

✓ Use templates for **quick responses** to repetitive requests.

How These Worksheets and Checklists Help

- Supervisors will **analyze their current time usage** and identify inefficiencies.
- They will apply the **Eisenhower Matrix** to **prioritize tasks effectively.**
- **Time-blocking strategies** will help **allocate time to high-impact work.**
- **Checklists will ensure ongoing accountability** and help supervisors **reduce interruptions, delegate effectively, and balance team priorities.**

Final Thought: Time is Your Most Valuable Asset

Time is the one resource you can never get back—how you invest it will define your success as a supervisor. **Every decision about your time is a decision about your impact.** The difference between feeling overwhelmed and being in control isn't about doing more—it's about doing the right things at the right time.

Mastering time and priorities isn't about squeezing every second out of the day; it's about **aligning your focus with what truly matters**—leading your team effectively, making strategic decisions, and fostering long-term growth.

Remember: **The best supervisors don't just manage time—they lead with intention.** Start implementing these strategies today, and you'll not only improve your efficiency but also create a more engaged, productive, and empowered team.

Your leadership journey isn't about keeping busy—it's about making an impact. Choose wisely.

Chapter 5: Delegating Effectively

Worksheet 1: Identifying Delegation Opportunities

Purpose: To assess your current workload and identify tasks that can and should be delegated.

Step 1: Audit Your Current Responsibilities

List **all** of the tasks you handle in a typical week. Be specific.

Task	Importance (High/Medium/Low)	Requires my expertise? (Yes/No)	Could be delegated? (Yes/No)
Example: Approving expense reports	Low	No	Yes
Example: Developing a training program	High	Yes	No

Step 2: Identify Tasks to Delegate

Review the table and list **at least three** tasks you can delegate immediately.
Task 1:

Task 2:

Task 3:

For each task, note why you selected it for delegation:

_____

_____

_____

Worksheet 2: Matching Tasks to Team Members

Purpose: To ensure delegation aligns with the strengths, interests, and development needs of team members.

Step 1: Assess Your Team

Fill out the following **Team Delegation Matrix**:

Team member	Strengths and skills	Areas for development	Tasks they could own
Example: James	Data analysis, reporting	Public speaking	Presenting key findings in meetings
Example: Maria	Project coordination	Financial forecasting	Assisting with quarterly budgeting

Who is best suited for the tasks you listed in Worksheet 1?

1. **Task:** _____ → **Team Member:** _____
2. **Task:** _____ → **Team Member:** _____
3. **Task:** _____ → **Team Member:** _____

Worksheet 3: Structuring the Delegation Process

Purpose: To ensure that expectations, timelines, and accountability measures are clearly communicated.

Step 1: Define the Delegation Details

For each task you plan to delegate, complete this table:

Task	Assigned to	Expected outcome	Deadline	Check-in points
Example: Managing weekly reports	James	Summarized data report to leadership	Every Friday	Midweek review

For each task, answer these key delegation questions:

1. **What is the specific desired outcome?**

   _____

2. **What resources or training does the employee need?**

   _____

3. **What level of authority will they have? (Full autonomy, partial decision making, consult for approval, and so on.)**

   _____

Worksheet 4: Avoiding Micromanagement and Building Trust

Purpose: To ensure that delegation is effective without unnecessary oversight.

Step 1: Self-Check—Are You Micromanaging?

Mark whether you exhibit these behaviors when delegating:

- ☐ I frequently check in on progress multiple times a day.
- ☐ I feel the need to correct small details rather than focusing on the outcome.
- ☐ I redo or "fix" work after it's submitted instead of providing feedback.
- ☐ I hesitate to delegate because I think "it's just easier to do it myself."
- ☐ I often take back tasks after assigning them.
- ☐ I rarely give employees the authority to make decisions.

If you checked three or more boxes, you may need to adjust your delegation style.

Step 2: Strategies to Build Trust Identify one action you can take to empower your team instead of micromanaging:

_____

_____

_____

Checklist: Effective Delegation Steps

Before Delegating

✓ **Identify the right task to delegate** (must be appropriate for the employee's skill level).

✓ **Choose the best person for the task** (consider strengths, career goals, and workload).

✓ Define the expected outcome clearly (what success looks like).

✓ **Decide on the level of autonomy** (how much decision-making authority they have).

During Delegation

✓ **Communicate expectations clearly** (goals, deadlines, and required standards).

✓ **Provide necessary resources** (tools, training, and contacts for support).

✓ **Schedule key check-in points** (avoid daily oversight, but ensure progress).

✓ **Give them the authority to act** (don't delegate responsibility without decision-making power).

After Delegation

✓ **Avoid jumping in to "fix" the work** (provide feedback instead).

✓ **Acknowledge the effort and results** (reinforce confidence and motivation).

✓ **Conduct a review session** (discuss what worked and what could improve for next time).

Reflection

Delegation Growth Plan

Which delegation habit do you need to improve most?

- ☐ Letting go of control
- ☐ Providing clearer expectations
- ☐ Avoiding micromanagement
- ☐ Delegating tasks that stretch employees' skills
- ☐ Following up effectively

One commitment I will make this week to improve my delegation skills:

_____

_____

_____

Final Thought: Great Leaders Build Great Teams

Delegation isn't just about distributing tasks—it's about **developing people**. Supervisors who delegate effectively **empower** their teams, create **opportunities for growth**, and **free themselves to focus on strategic leadership**. Remember, every task you delegate is an investment in your team's capability and your success as a leader.

Take **one step today**: delegate a task using the techniques outlined in this chapter and observe the impact. The strongest supervisors don't hold on to work—they **lift their teams up** by trusting them with responsibility. **Now, go delegate with confidence!**

Chapter 6: Resolving Conflicts and Handling Difficult Conversations

Worksheet 1: Identifying Conflict in Your Team

Purpose: To help supervisors recognize common sources of conflict within their teams before they escalate.

Step 1: Identifying Recent or Ongoing Conflicts: Think about your team's interactions over the past month. List any **disagreements, tensions, or ongoing issues** that have surfaced.

Conflict situation	Type of conflict (Interpersonal, task-related, organizational)	Impact on team (High/ Medium/ Low)	Addressed yet? (Yes/No)
Example: Disagreement on project deadlines	Task-Related	Medium	No
Example: Two team members avoiding communication	Interpersonal	High	Yes

Step 2: Reflection on Unresolved Conflicts

Choose one conflict from your list that **hasn't been fully addressed** and answer the following questions:

1. **What is the core issue behind this conflict?**

   _____

2. **How is it affecting team dynamics, performance, or morale?**

   _____

3. **What might happen if it remains unaddressed?**

   _____

4. **Who needs to be involved in resolving it?**

   _____

Worksheet 2: Diagnosing Conflict Using Emotional Intelligence

Purpose: To assess how emotional intelligence (EQ) plays a role in resolving workplace conflicts.

Step 1: Self-Assessment—How Well Do You Handle Conflict?

Rate yourself on a scale of **1 (Rarely) to 5 (Always)** for each of the following:

- ☐ I recognize my own emotional responses before reacting.
- ☐ I stay calm and composed when managing conflicts.
- ☐ I actively listen to different perspectives without interrupting.
- ☐ I acknowledge the emotions of others during disagreements.
- ☐ I separate personal feelings from professional decisions.
- ☐ I use conflict as an opportunity to strengthen relationships.

Step 2: Reflection on Emotional Triggers

Identify **one emotional trigger** that makes handling conflict difficult for you. (Example: defensiveness, frustration, avoidance)

My personal trigger: _____

How I can manage it effectively: _____
_____

Worksheet 3: Preparing for a Difficult Conversation

Purpose: To structure conversations before they happen, ensuring clarity and a productive outcome.

Step 1: Define the Situation: Answer these questions before initiating a conflict resolution conversation:

1. **What is the main issue I need to address?**

   _____

2. **What specific examples can I use to illustrate the issue?**

   _____

3. **What outcome am I hoping to achieve?**

   _____

4. **What concerns might the other person have, and how can I address them?**

   _____

Step 2: Plan the Conversation Structure Use this Conflict Resolution Framework to outline your approach:

Step	Key talking points
1. Opening the Conversation	"I wanted to check in about [issue] because I've noticed [specific example]."
2. Acknowledging Perspectives	"I'd like to hear your perspective on this. Can you share how you see the situation?"
3. Identifying the Root Cause	"It seems like the challenge is [root cause]. Does that sound right to you?"
4. Collaborating on Solutions	"How do you think we can move forward in a way that works for both of us?"
5. Agreeing on Next Steps	"Let's agree on [solution]. I'll follow up with you in [timeframe] to check progress."

Step 3: Set the Tone for Success

- ☐ Choose a **neutral and private** setting for the conversation.
- ☐ Maintain open body language and a calm tone.
- ☐ Focus on facts, not emotions or assumptions.

Worksheet 4: Conflict Resolution Action Plan

Purpose: To ensure conflicts are resolved effectively with clear follow-up.

Step 1: Document Agreed Solutions Use this table to track agreements reached during conflict resolution conversations.

Conflict	Agreed solution	Who is responsible?	Deadline for action	Follow-up date
Example: Dispute over project roles	Redefine responsibilities and clarify ownership in writing	Sarah & John	End of this week	Next Monday

Step 2: Follow-Up Questions One week after resolving the conflict, check in by answering the following:

1. **Has the solution been implemented? If not, why?**

   _____

2. **Has the conflict resurfaced in any way?**

   _____

3. **What adjustments (if any) are needed to maintain a positive outcome?**

   _____

Checklist: Essential Conflict Resolution Steps

Before the Conversation

✓ **Recognize signs of conflict early** (changes in behavior, tension, avoidance).

✓ **Determine if intervention is necessary** (is this conflict affecting performance or morale?).

✓ **Prepare specific examples of the issue** (avoid vague accusations).

✓ **Choose a neutral setting and appropriate timing.**

During the Conversation

✓ **Stay calm, composed, and focused on resolution.**

✓ **Acknowledge each person's perspective before proposing solutions.**

✓ **Encourage open and honest communication.**

✓ **Guide the conversation toward actionable next steps.**

After the Conversation

✓ **Document key agreements** (who is responsible for what?).

✓ **Follow up to ensure changes are being implemented.**

✓ **Recognize improvements and encourage continued collaboration.**

✓ **Reflect on lessons learned for handling future conflicts more effectively.**

Reflection: Conflict Management Growth Plan

Purpose: To ensure continuous improvement in conflict resolution skills.

Step 1: Identify Areas for Improvement Which conflict resolution skill do you need to work on most?

☐ Staying calm under pressure
☐ Actively listening without interrupting
☐ Addressing conflicts sooner rather than later

☐ Being more direct in difficult conversations

☐ Encouraging team members to resolve conflicts independently

Step 2: Action Commitment One commitment I will make this week to improve my conflict resolution approach:

_____

_____

_____

Final Thought: Conflict is an Opportunity, Not a Threat

Handling conflict isn't about "winning" or "losing"—it's about **understanding, collaboration, and growth**. The strongest supervisors don't eliminate conflict—they **navigate it skillfully** to strengthen relationships, improve processes, and build more resilient teams.

Your challenge for this week: **Identify one workplace tension** and use the techniques in this chapter to address it proactively. Whether it's a small miscommunication or a brewing dispute, practicing **calm, structured conflict resolution** will prepare you for bigger leadership challenges ahead.

Chapter 7: Supporting Team Development and Growth

Worksheet 1: Identifying Development Needs

Purpose: To assess team members' current skills, career goals, and areas for growth.

Step 1: Employee Skills and Development Assessment List your team members and their current skills, career aspirations, and development needs.

Employee name	Strengths & skills	Career aspirations	Development needs	Growth opportunities
Example: Alex	Strong project management	Wants to move into leadership	Needs public speaking practice	Present in team meetings

Step 2: Identifying Development Gaps

Answer the following for each employee:

1. **What are their strongest skills?**

   _____

2. **What areas need improvement for their current role?**

   _____

3. **What skills will they need for future career aspirations?**

   _____

4. **What opportunities can I provide to help them grow?**

   _____

Worksheet 2: Creating an Individualized Development Plan (IDP)

Purpose: To create a structured roadmap for each employee's growth.

Step 1: Employee Goal-Setting Work with each employee to set SMART development goals (Specific, Measurable, Achievable, Relevant, Time-bound).

Development goal	Skills needed	Action steps	Deadline	Support needed
Example: Improve presentation skills	Public speaking, storytelling	Enroll in online course, practice presentations at meetings	3 months	Supervisor feedback, mentor guidance

Step 2: Tracking Progress Plan quarterly check-ins to review development progress.

Check-in date	Progress achieved	Adjustments needed?	Next steps
Example: April 10	Completed public speaking course	Needs more real-world practice	Present at department meeting

Worksheet 3: Growth Opportunity Map

Purpose: To identify on-the-job development opportunities for each team member.

Step 1: Growth Opportunity Identification: Match current work opportunities with development needs.

Development need	On-the-job growth opportunity	Expected benefit
Improve leadership skills	Lead a cross-functional project	Gain real experience in team leadership
Build technical skills	Work on a high-profile tech project	Hands-on exposure to key technologies

Step 2: Assigning Stretch Assignments: Identify real projects where employees can develop new skills.

1. **What projects or tasks can be delegated for skill development?**

   _____

2. **Which employees are ready for leadership roles or additional responsibility?**

   _____

3. **How can I ensure they receive the right support and feedback?**

   _____

Worksheet 4: Fostering a Growth Mindset in the Team

Purpose: To encourage continuous learning and a culture of development.

Step 1: Encouraging Learning and Development: Check off the strategies you already use and highlight new ones to implement.

- ✓ I encourage employees to take ownership of their own growth.
- ✓ I provide constructive feedback focused on improvement.
- ✓ I support learning from mistakes rather than punishing them.
- ✓ I share my own learning experiences and mistakes.
- ✓ I provide access to training resources and mentorship.
- ✓ I celebrate small learning milestones, not just big achievements.

Step 2: Growth Mindset Coaching During team meetings or 1:1 sessions, ask employees:

1. What's one new thing you learned this week?
2. What challenge did you face, and what did you learn from it?
3. What's something outside your comfort zone you want to try?

Worksheet 5: Creating a Culture of Feedback and Recognition

Purpose: To integrate regular feedback and recognition into development efforts.

Step 1: Structuring Developmental Feedback: Use the SBI Model (situation, behavior, impact) to provide feedback that promotes growth.

Situation	Behavior	Impact	Improvement suggestion
Example: During last week's team meeting	Spoke confidently but didn't engage the audience	The message was clear, but team members didn't participate	Use open-ended questions to invite discussion

Step 2: Recognizing Growth and Achievements How often do you recognize your employees' development progress?

✓ **Daily (small verbal acknowledgments)**
✓ **Weekly (team shout-outs, e-mail recognition)**
✓ **Monthly (formal reviews, bonuses, promotions)**
✓ **Quarterly (development plan check-ins, public recognition)**

Checklist: Supervisor's Guide to Supporting Team Growth

Daily Development Habits

✓ Encourage continuous learning and curiosity.
✓ Provide opportunities for employees to stretch and challenge themselves.
✓ Recognize and celebrate small growth milestones.
✓ Offer real-time feedback that reinforces positive behaviors.

Weekly Development Practices

✓ Hold informal one-on-one check-ins to discuss development.
✓ Delegate small leadership or skill-building opportunities.
✓ Encourage peer mentoring or knowledge-sharing sessions.
✓ Support employees in setting learning goals for the week.

Monthly Development Strategies

✓ Review Individualized Development Plans (IDPs) for progress.
✓ Assign stretch assignments aligned with career aspirations.
✓ Connect employees with mentors or networking opportunities.
✓ Recognize employees for their growth and contributions.

Quarterly and Annual Development Initiatives

✓ Conduct structured performance and development reviews.
✓ Offer professional development training, courses, or certifications.
✓ Adjust and refine IDPs based on evolving skills and aspirations.
✓ Advocate for employee promotions, job rotations, or career advancements.

Reflection: Your Role in Team Development

Purpose: To reflect on your own impact as a supervisor in fostering team growth.

Step 1: Assess Your Coaching Style: How would you describe your approach to employee development?

☐ Hands-off (employees are responsible for their own growth)
☐ Supportive (I encourage development but let employees take the lead)
☐ Hands-on (I actively guide employees through their growth plans)
☐ A mix of supportive and hands-on coaching

Step 2: Action Commitment One specific commitment I will make to improve how I support my team's development:

_____

_____

Step 3: Growth Mindset Reminder ✓ I will view challenges as opportunities for learning.

✓ **I will encourage my team to embrace continuous improvement.**
✓ **I will support employees in reaching their full potential.**

_____

Final Thought: The Supervisor's Legacy

As a supervisor, your greatest impact isn't measured by how much you accomplish yourself—it's measured by how much you help others grow. When you **invest in your team's development, you're shaping the future leaders of your organization.**

Your challenge this week: **Choose one team member and identify a specific growth opportunity** to support their development. Whether it's assigning a stretch project, enrolling them in a training program, or simply having a career discussion, take one step toward cultivating a stronger, more capable team.

Chapter 8: Navigating Change and Uncertainty

Worksheet 1: Understanding Change Readiness

Purpose: Assess your team's current mindset and preparedness for change.

Step 1: Team Readiness Assessment

Rate your team's current level of **change readiness** on a scale of **1 (Not Ready) to 5 (Highly Ready)**.

Factor	1 Not ready	2 Slightly ready	3 Somewhat ready	4 Mostly ready	5 Highly ready
Adapts well to new processes	☐	☐	☐	☐	☐
Communicates openly about change	☐	☐	☐	☐	☐
Trusts leadership during transitions	☐	☐	☐	☐	☐
Sees change as an opportunity rather than a threat	☐	☐	☐	☐	☐
Has a strong learning and growth mindset	☐	☐	☐	☐	☐

Step 2: Identifying Potential Resistance

Ask yourself:

1. **Who on my team is most likely to resist this change?**

   _____

2. **What concerns might they have?**

   _____

3. **How can I proactively address these concerns?**

   _____

_____

Worksheet 2: Crafting a Change Communication Plan

Purpose: Develop a clear, structured communication strategy to guide your team through change.

Step 1: Define the Message Using the "What-Why-How" Framework

1. **What is changing?** (Be clear and specific)

   _____

2. **Why is this change happening?** (Explain the reasoning)

   _____

3. **How will this change impact my team?**

   _____

4. **What support is available to help them adapt?**

   _____

Step 2: Choose Communication Methods

- ✓ **Team meetings** for major updates
- ✓ **One-on-one check-ins** for individual concerns
- ✓ **E-mail updates** for consistency
- ✓ **Feedback sessions** to gather input

Step 3: Plan the Frequency of Communication

Communication type	Frequency	Notes
Initial Announcement	//___	Set expectations clearly
Team Check-ins	Weekly/Biweekly	Address concerns, reinforce support
Progress Updates	Every ___ weeks	Provide measurable updates
Feedback Sessions	Monthly	Adjust strategies based on input

Worksheet 3: Managing Resistance to Change

Purpose: Identify resistance and develop strategies to turn opposition into engagement.

Step 1: Identify Resistance Types

Check all that apply to your team:
- ✓ **Logical resistance** (concerns about feasibility, resources, workload)
- ✓ **Emotional resistance** (fear of the unknown, loss of control, anxiety)
- ✓ **Personal resistance** (worry about job security, career impact)

Step 2: Develop responses to resistance: For each type of resistance, develop a strategy to address and mitigate concerns.

Resistance type	Example concern	Supervisor response
Logical	"This will add too much to our workload."	Adjust workloads, explain efficiency benefits, provide additional support.
Emotional	"I'm worried I won't be able to adapt."	Offer training, provide mentorship, reinforce past successes.
Personal	"Will I still have a place in this team?"	Clarify role adjustments, highlight growth opportunities.

Worksheet 4: Creating Stability During Change

Purpose: Identify ways to maintain team confidence and morale through uncertain transitions.

Step 1: Identify What Can Remain Stable

Even during change, some elements **should remain constant** to provide a sense of stability. Identify what can stay the same for your team:

- ✓ Team meeting schedules
- ✓ Recognition programs
- ✓ Certain workflows or responsibilities
- ✓ Manager availability for support

Step 2: Balance Stability with Adaptability

For each change, **find a way to reinforce stability**.

Change	What's staying the same?	How to reinforce stability
New software implementation	Our customer service process	Highlight improvements and offer training.
Team restructuring	Employee career growth opportunities	Reaffirm individual contributions and growth plans.

Worksheet 5: Leading with Emotional Intelligence During Change

Purpose: Use emotional intelligence (EQ) to guide your team through uncertainty.

Step 1: Assess Your Emotional Intelligence (EQ) Strengths

Rate yourself on a scale of **1 (Needs Work)** to **5 (Strongest Skill)**.

EQ skill	1 Needs work	2 Developing	3 Neutral	4 Good	5 Strong
Self-awareness (Understanding my own emotions)	☐	☐	☐	☐	☐
Self-regulation (Staying calm under pressure)	☐	☐	☐	☐	☐
Empathy (Understanding how my team feels)	☐	☐	☐	☐	☐
Social skills (Effectively leading conversations)	☐	☐	☐	☐	☐

Step 2: Emotional Intelligence Action Plan

Choose **one EQ skill** to improve during change.

- **Skill to focus on:** _____
- **Action I will take:** _____
- **How I will measure improvement:** _____

_____

Checklist: Supervisor's Guide to Navigating Change

Before the Change Begins

✓ Understand the change fully before communicating it to my team.
✓ Assess potential resistance and develop mitigation strategies.
✓ Prepare a clear, structured communication plan.
✓ Identify key team members who can help champion the change.

During the Change Process

✓ Maintain regular and transparent communication.
✓ Check in with employees individually to address concerns.
✓ Monitor morale and look for signs of stress or resistance.
✓ Reinforce stability by keeping key team routines in place.
✓ Recognize and celebrate small wins to build momentum.

After the Change is Implemented

✓ Evaluate what worked well and what could be improved.
✓ Gather feedback from employees on their experience.
✓ Provide ongoing support to ensure long-term success.
✓ Recognize employees who adapted well and contributed to the transition.

Reflection: Your Change Leadership Approach

Purpose: Reflect on your approach and prepare for future changes.

Step 1: Self-Assessment of Change Leadership

How do I typically handle change?
☐ I embrace it and see it as an opportunity.
☐ I adjust but with some hesitation.
☐ I find it challenging and stressful.

Step 2: Identify One Area for Improvement

One thing I can do to improve my leadership during change:

Step 3: Commitment to Continuous Learning

✓ **I will seek feedback from my team on how I handled this
change.**
✓ **I will learn more about change management strategies.**
✓ **I will reflect on my own responses to change and adjust as
needed.**

Final Thought: The Supervisor as a Change Navigator

Great supervisors **don't just react to change—they lead it.** By preparing in advance, communicating effectively, and supporting employees
through uncertainty, you can **turn resistance into resilience and change
into opportunity.**

Your challenge this week: **Identify one upcoming change in your organization and create a proactive plan to guide your team through it.**

Chapter 9: Hiring Right: The Role of a Supervisor in Building a Team

Worksheet 1: Defining the Hiring Criteria

Purpose: Identify the key attributes, skills, and cultural fit required for the role.

Step 1: Role-Specific Needs Assessment

Fill in the table below to clarify what you are looking for in a candidate.

Category	Essential requirements	Nice-to-have qualities
Technical Skills	_____	_____
Soft Skills (e.g., communication, teamwork)	_____	_____
Experience Level	_____	_____
Cultural Fit (values, work style)	_____	_____
Adaptability & Learning Ability	_____	_____

Step 2: Team Integration Considerations

• What gaps exist in my current team that this new hire should help fill?

_____

• What qualities will ensure this person enhances team dynamics rather than disrupts them?

_____

• How will I assess cultural fit during the hiring process?

_____
_____

Worksheet 2: Crafting the Job Description

Purpose: Develop a clear and effective job description to attract the right candidates.

Step 1: Job Posting Blueprint

Fill in the following sections to draft a compelling job description.

Job Title: _____

Department: _____

Reports To: _____

Key Responsibilities:

- _____
- _____
- _____

Required Qualifications:

✓ _____
✓ _____
✓ _____

Preferred Qualifications:

✓ _____
✓ _____
✓ _____

Key Success Indicators in the First 90 Days:

✓ _____
✓ _____
✓ _____

Step 2: Screening for the Right Candidates

Before posting the job, check the following:

✓ Job description accurately reflects team needs and role expectations.
✓ The language is inclusive and free of unintentional bias.
✓ The posting is clear about responsibilities, expectations, and opportunities for growth.

Worksheet 3: Interview Planning and Question Bank

Purpose: Develop a structured interview process that evaluates candidates fairly and consistently.

Step 1: Create an Interview Structure

✓ **Phone Screen (15–20 minutes):** Initial candidate fit & basic qualifications

✓ **First Interview (30–45 minutes):** Deeper skill & experience assessment

✓ **Second Interview (45–60 minutes):** Cultural fit, team dynamics, and behavioral questions

✓ **Final Interview (if needed):** Leadership/team meet-and-greet

Step 2: Develop Behavioral Interview Questions

✓ **Problem Solving and Critical Thinking:**

"Tell me about a time you had to solve a complex problem with limited information. What was your approach?"

✓ **Collaboration and Teamwork:**

"Describe a situation where you had to work closely with someone whose personality or work style differed from yours. How did you manage it?"

✓ **Handling Conflict:**

"Give me an example of a time you had a disagreement with a coworker or manager. How did you resolve it?"

✓ **Adaptability and Learning:**

"Tell me about a time you had to quickly learn a new skill or adapt to a major change in your job."

✓ **Cultural Fit and Values:**

"What type of work environment brings out your best performance? Can you describe a time when a workplace culture either helped or hindered your success?"

Worksheet 4: Assessing Candidate Fit

Purpose: Compare candidates objectively using a structured evaluation process.

Step 1: Candidate Scorecard

Rate candidates from **1 (Poor) to 5 (Excellent)** in each category.

Candidate name:

_____	**Candidate 1**	**Candidate 2**	**Candidate 3**
Technical Skills			
Communication Skills			
Cultural Fit			
Problem-Solving Ability			
Team Dynamics			

Total Scores:
Candidate 1: _____
Candidate 2: _____
Candidate 3: _____

Step 2: Final Decision Considerations

- ✓ **Who aligns best with our long-term team goals?**
- ✓ **Which candidate will adapt and grow in the role?**
- ✓ **Who demonstrates a balance of skills, personality, and team chemistry?**

Checklist: The Hiring Process from Start to Finish

Before Posting the Job

✓ Define key skills, attributes, and experience required.
✓ Write a clear, engaging, and unbiased job description.
✓ Determine who will be involved in the hiring process.

During the Hiring Process

✓ Use structured interview questions to assess candidates fairly.
✓ Have multiple team members participate in interviews for a well-rounded perspective.
✓ Test for technical and soft skills using real-world scenarios.

After the Interviews

✓ Compare candidates using the structured evaluation method.
✓ Conduct reference checks before making an offer.
✓ Ensure the offer is competitive and clearly outlines expectations.

Onboarding for Success

✓ Create a structured onboarding plan (30-60-90 day roadmap).
✓ Assign a mentor or buddy to help the new hire integrate.
✓ Set clear performance expectations and schedule regular check-ins.
✓ Celebrate small wins and reinforce positive behaviors early.

Reflection: Supervisor's Role in Hiring Right

Purpose: Evaluate your approach to hiring and identify areas for improvement.

Step 1: Self-Assessment

- What hiring challenges have I faced in the past?

  _____

- How can I improve my approach to hiring moving forward?

  _____

- What is one key takeaway I learned from this process?

  _____

Step 2: Commitment to Hiring Excellence

- ✓ **I will prioritize hiring for both skills and cultural fit.**
- ✓ **I will take the time needed to hire the right person rather than rush the process.**
- ✓ **I will ensure a structured onboarding experience to set new hires up for success.**

Final Thought: The Supervisor as a Team Builder

Great supervisors don't just fill positions—they **build high-performing teams**. Thoughtful hiring leads to stronger teams, better workplace dynamics, and long-term success.

Your challenge this week: **Review your team's current hiring needs and refine your hiring process using the worksheets above.**

Chapter 10: Understanding Performance Management and Accountability

Worksheet 1: Defining Performance Expectations

Purpose: Set clear performance expectations to ensure alignment between supervisors and employees.

Step 1: Define Key Responsibilities

List the primary responsibilities for a specific role to establish a baseline for performance expectations.

Key responsibility	Expected outcome	Performance metric
_____	_____	_____
_____	_____	_____
_____	_____	_____

Step 2: Setting SMART Goals

Create **Specific, Measurable, Achievable, Relevant, and Time-bound (SMART)** goals for each employee.

✓ **Example:** Instead of saying, "Improve customer service," use:

"Reduce average customer wait time from 5 minutes to 3 minutes by the end of Q2 through improved process efficiency."

Now, define **three SMART goals** for a team member:

1. _____
2. _____
3. _____

Step 3: Aligning Goals with Team and Organizational Objectives

✓ How do these goals contribute to the company's overall mission?
✓ What resources or support does the employee need to achieve them?

Worksheet 2: Structuring Feedback for Growth

Purpose: Provide regular and constructive feedback to foster development.

Step 1: Prepare for a Feedback Conversation

✓ Identify the purpose of the feedback:
✓ Is it positive reinforcement or constructive improvement?
✓ What specific behaviors or actions are being addressed?
✓ What outcome are you hoping to achieve?

Step 2: Using the SBI (Situation-Behavior-Impact) Feedback Model

✓ **Situation:** Describe when and where the event occurred.
✓ **Behavior:** Explain what the employee did (focus on actions, not personality).
✓ **Impact:** Share the result of their actions on the team, customer, or business.
✓ **Example SBI Feedback:**

"Sara, during yesterday's client meeting (Situation), you proactively answered the customer's concerns with well-researched insights (Behavior). This reassured the client and helped secure the contract (Impact)."

Now, write feedback for a recent employee action using the SBI model:

Situation: _____

Behavior: _____

Impact: _____

Step 3: Encourage a Two-Way Conversation

✓ Ask the employee for their perspective: "How do you feel about your performance in this area?"
✓ Discuss solutions together: "What steps do you think will help improve this?"

Worksheet 3: Performance Check-In

Purpose: Maintain ongoing performance conversations rather than relying solely on annual reviews.

Step 1: Schedule Regular One-on-Ones

- ✓ How often will check-ins be held? ☐ Weekly ☐ Bi-weekly ☐ Monthly
- ✓ Preferred format? ☐ In-person ☐ Virtual ☐ E-mail summary

Step 2: One-on-One Discussion Framework

Discussion area	Notes
Wins since the last check-in	_____
Challenges & obstacles	_____
Progress on goals	_____
Skills development opportunities	_____
Supervisor support needed	_____

Step 3: Employee Self-Reflection

- ✓ What are you most proud of in your work over the past month?
- ✓ What challenges have you faced, and how did you handle them?
- ✓ What skills or resources do you need to perform at your best?

Worksheet 4: Addressing Performance Issues

Purpose: Manage performance concerns constructively and proactively.

Step 1: Identify Performance Gaps

Performance concern	Expected standard	Observed behavior
_____	_____	_____
_____	_____	_____
_____	_____	_____

Step 2: Craft an Improvement Plan (Use the PIP Method— Performance Improvement Plan)

✓ Define the Issue Clearly:

_____

✓ Set Measurable Goals for Improvement:

_____

✓ Provide Support (Training, Coaching, Resources):

_____

✓ Establish Timelines for Progress Checks:

_____

Step 3: Follow Up with Accountability Measures

✓ Regular check-ins scheduled? ☐ Yes ☐ No
✓ Progress milestones established? ☐ Yes ☐ No
✓ Employee acknowledges expectations? ☐ Yes ☐ No

Worksheet 5: The Formal Performance Review

Purpose: Conduct effective and well-prepared performance evaluations.

Step 1: Employee Self-Assessment

✓ What accomplishments are you most proud of this year?
✓ What challenges did you face, and how did you overcome them?
✓ What feedback would you like from your supervisor to improve further?

Step 2: Supervisor Evaluation Categories

Rate the employee's performance in key areas (1 = Needs Improvement, 5 = Excellent).

Category	1	2	3	4	5
Quality of Work	☐	☐	☐	☐	☐
Communication	☐	☐	☐	☐	☐
Problem Solving	☐	☐	☐	☐	☐
Team Collaboration	☐	☐	☐	☐	☐
Accountability	☐	☐	☐	☐	☐

Step 3: Establish Growth Goals for the Next Review Period

✓ What specific areas should the employee improve?
✓ What new responsibilities or leadership opportunities can be given?
✓ How will success be measured?

Checklist: Ensuring a Culture of Accountability

Purpose: Keep performance management fair, transparent, and continuous.

Setting Expectations

✓ Have I clearly communicated performance expectations to my team?

✓ Do employees understand how their work contributes to the organization's success?

✓ Are team members involved in setting their own performance goals?

Providing Regular Feedback

✓ Am I giving both positive and constructive feedback frequently?

✓ Do I use a structured approach like SBI or the Start-Stop-Continue method?

✓ Do employees feel comfortable receiving and giving feedback?

Managing Underperformance

✓ Have I identified performance issues early rather than waiting for formal reviews?

✓ Have I provided necessary coaching, resources, or training?

✓ Have I documented performance conversations and set measurable improvement plans?

Encouraging Employee Development

✓ Am I offering opportunities for employees to develop skills and grow?

✓ Do I regularly discuss career progression with my team members?

✓ Have I recognized employee achievements publicly and meaningfully?

Ensuring Fair and Effective Reviews

- ✓ Do I conduct performance evaluations consistently and without bias?
- ✓ Are formal reviews based on data, observations, and documented feedback?
- ✓ Are performance reviews followed up with a development plan for the employee?

Reflection: Supervisor's Performance Management Philosophy

Purpose: Reflect on your role in fostering performance and accountability.

Step 1: Self-Assessment for Supervisors

- ✓ Am I providing clear, actionable feedback to my employees?
- ✓ Do I balance accountability with support and encouragement?
- ✓ Am I actively working to build a culture of trust and development?

Step 2: Identify Areas for Growth

- ✓ What is one aspect of performance management I can improve?
- ✓ How can I better support my team in reaching their goals?
- ✓ What is one change I will implement in my next feedback conversation?

Final Thought: The Supervisor as a Performance Leader

Supervisors who embrace **clear expectations, continuous feedback, and accountability** create teams that perform at their best. **Your challenge: Implement at least one new performance management practice from this chapter and track its impact on your team.**

Chapter 11: Leading with Empathy and Allowing Space to Fail

Worksheet 1: Developing Your Empathy as a Leader

Purpose: Self-assess and improve your ability to lead with empathy.

Step 1: Reflect on Your Leadership Approach

✓ How do I typically respond when an employee makes a mistake?

✓ Do I focus more on blame or learning?

✓ How comfortable do I feel discussing emotions and challenges with my team?

✓ When was the last time I admitted a mistake to my team? What was the outcome?

Step 2: Strengthening Empathy Through Active Listening

✓ Think of a recent conversation where an employee shared a challenge. Did you:

Listen without interrupting?
Ask follow-up questions to understand their perspective?
Reflect back what they said to confirm understanding?
Avoid immediately jumping to solutions or fixing the problem?

Action Plan:

✓ How can I improve my active listening skills?

_____

✓ What is one action I will take in my next one-on-one meeting to demonstrate empathy?

_____

Worksheet 2: Creating a Safe Space for Failure

Purpose: Establish an environment where employees feel comfortable taking risks and learning from mistakes.

Step 1: Assess Your Current Team Culture

✓ Do my employees feel comfortable admitting mistakes? ☐ Yes ☐ No
✓ Do team members support each other in problem solving?
  ☐ Yes ☐ No
✓ When mistakes happen, does the team focus on solutions rather than blame? ☐ Yes ☐ No

Step 2: Encouraging Psychological Safety

✓ Have I explicitly told my team that mistakes are learning opportunities? ☐ Yes ☐ No
✓ Have I shared examples of my own mistakes and what I learned from them? ☐ Yes ☐ No
✓ Do I encourage open discussions about challenges without fear of punishment? ☐ Yes ☐ No

Step 3: Implementing a Fail-Fast, Learn-Fast Mindset

✓ How will I reframe mistakes as learning opportunities?
✓ What specific language will I use when addressing team mistakes?

Example Reframing Statements:

Instead of: "This is unacceptable." → Try: "Let's analyze what happened and see what we can improve."

Instead of: "Who's responsible for this error?" → Try: "What can we learn from this experience?"

Worksheet 3: Turning Mistakes Into Learning Opportunities

Purpose: Guide employees through failure in a way that promotes growth.

Step 1: Conduct a Post-Failure Reflection

✓ Describe the situation (What happened?):

_____

✓ **Identify the root cause** (Why did it happen?):

_____

✓ **Analyze the impact** (What were the consequences?):

_____

✓ **Extract key lessons** (What did we learn?):

_____

✓ **Develop an action plan** (How will we prevent this in the future?):

_____

Step 2: Encourage Team Reflection

✓ What worked well despite the mistake?
✓ What would we do differently next time?
✓ How can we support each other in improving?

Step 3: Apply the Lessons Learned

✓ What concrete changes will we implement based on this experience?
✓ How will we track improvements over time?

_____

Worksheet 4: Balancing Accountability with Support

Purpose: Ensure that employees learn from mistakes while maintaining accountability.

Step 1: Define the Nature of the Mistake

✓ Was this mistake due to:

A lack of knowledge or training?
A miscommunication?
An oversight or carelessness?
External factors beyond the employee's control?

Step 2: Choose the Right Response

Situation	Supervisor response
Lack of knowledge or training	Provide additional training or mentorship
Miscommunication	Clarify expectations and improve communication
Oversight or carelessness	Discuss attention to detail and reinforce accountability
External factors	Identify process improvements and systemic changes

Step 3: Providing Constructive Support

✓ Did I communicate expectations clearly? ☐ Yes ☐ No
✓ Have I given the employee an opportunity to correct the mistake? ☐ Yes ☐ No
✓ Have I provided the necessary resources and support? ☐ Yes ☐ No

Step 4: Follow Up and Monitor Progress

✓ How will I check in on the employee's improvement?
✓ What support will I offer moving forward?

Worksheet 5: Encouraging Innovation and Risk-Taking

Purpose: Help employees feel safe to experiment and try new ideas.

Step 1: Assess Risk-Taking in Your Team

✓ Do employees feel comfortable sharing new ideas? ☐ Yes ☐ No
✓ Are risks encouraged, even when they lead to failure? ☐ Yes ☐ No
✓ Are employees rewarded for creative problem solving? ☐ Yes ☐ No

Step 2: Encouraging Experimentation

✓ What new initiative or experiment can I encourage my team to try?
✓ How will I reassure employees that failure is part of the process?

Step 3: Celebrating Learning from Failure

✓ Have I publicly recognized employees who took a risk, even if it didn't work? ☐ Yes ☐ No
✓ What success stories can I share that resulted from past failures?

Checklist: Creating an Empathy-Driven Leadership Approach

Purpose: Ensure you're actively leading with empathy in daily interactions.

Personal Reflection as a Leader

✓ Have I made an effort to understand my employees' perspectives?

✓ Do I check in on employees' well-being beyond work tasks?

✓ Have I openly shared my own challenges or mistakes to normalize learning?

Daily Practices for Empathetic Leadership

✓ Listen actively and without judgment.

✓ Show appreciation for employees' efforts, even when results aren't perfect.

✓ Avoid jumping to conclusions—seek to understand before responding.

✓ Provide support rather than criticism when mistakes happen.

✓ Regularly ask: "How can I help you succeed?"

Fostering Psychological Safety in the Team

✓ Create an environment where employees feel safe expressing concerns.

✓ Encourage team members to ask for help without fear of judgment.

✓ Reinforce that mistakes are part of growth, not failures to be punished.

✓ Use team meetings to openly discuss lessons learned from mistakes.

Encouraging a Learning Culture

✓ Recognize and reward employees who take initiative, even if outcomes are imperfect.

✓ Host team "retrospectives" to reflect on what went well and what can improve.

✓ Invest in employee development through coaching, training, and mentorship.

✓ Demonstrate patience and support when employees struggle with new tasks.

Final Reflection: Your Leadership Commitment

Purpose: Define the actions you will take to lead with empathy and allow space for failure.

Step 1: Identify Your Key Takeaway

✓ What is one lesson from this chapter that resonated most with me?

Step 2: Set a Leadership Intention

✓ How will I demonstrate empathy in my leadership this week?

Step 3: Take Action

✓ One immediate step I will take to create a failure-friendly environment:

Final Thought: The Supervisor as a Growth Catalyst

Supervisors who **lead with empathy and embrace failure as a tool for learning** create resilient, engaged teams. **Your challenge:** Implement at least one new practice from this chapter and observe how it changes your team's confidence, creativity, and problem-solving abilities.

Chapter 12: Becoming a Continuous Learner: Supervisor for Life

Worksheet 1: *Assessing Your Growth Mindset*

Purpose: Identify areas where you can adopt a stronger growth mindset.

Step 1: Self-Reflection

✓ Do I see challenges as opportunities to grow rather than obstacles to avoid? □ Yes □ No

✓ Do I embrace feedback, even when it's critical? □ Yes □ No

✓ Do I believe my leadership abilities can improve with effort and learning? □ Yes □ No

✓ How do I react when I make a mistake?

I feel discouraged and avoid similar situations in the future.
I analyze what went wrong and look for ways to improve.

✓ When faced with something I don't know, do I:

Avoid it and focus on what I'm already good at?
Seek out learning opportunities to develop new skills?

Step 2: Identify Areas for Growth

✓ What leadership skills do I need to improve?
✓ How can I shift my mindset to be more open to learning?

Action Plan:

✓ One thing I will do this month to develop my growth mindset:

Worksheet 2: Setting a Learning Goal

Purpose: Create a structured plan for continuous learning.

Step 1: Define Your Learning Focus

✓ What leadership skill do I want to improve?
✓ Why is this skill important for my role?
✓ How will improving this skill benefit my team?

Step 2: Choose Your Learning Method

✓ Which method(s) will I use to build this skill?

Online courses
Books
Podcasts
Peer mentoring
Formal workshops
Job shadowing

Step 3: Set a SMART Learning Goal

✓ **Specific**: What exactly will I learn?
✓ **Measurable**: How will I track my progress?
✓ **Achievable**: Do I have the time/resources to do this?
✓ **Relevant**: How does this align with my supervisory role?
✓ **Time-bound**: When will I complete this goal?

Step 4: Implementation Plan

✓ What are the first three steps I need to take?
✓ How will I stay accountable?
✓ Who can support or mentor me in this process?

Worksheet 3: Learning from Your Team

Purpose: Use your team's knowledge to grow as a leader.

Step 1: Identifying Knowledge Sources

✓ Who on my team has knowledge or skills that I can learn from?
✓ What expertise do my team members have that I lack?
✓ How can I encourage my team to share their knowledge with me and each other?

Step 2: Creating Opportunities for Peer Learning

✓ How often do I ask my team for their input and insights?

Rarely
Sometimes
Often

✓ Have I set up a system for my team to share best practices?
  ☐ Yes ☐ No
✓ What's one way I can learn from my team this month?

Step 3: Learning from Team Challenges

✓ Think of a recent team challenge or mistake.
✓ What did I learn from that experience?
✓ How can I use that lesson to improve my leadership?

Worksheet 4: *Expanding Your Learning Network*

Purpose: Connect with other supervisors and professionals to accelerate learning.

Step 1: Identify Learning Resources

✓ Which professional networks or associations am I part of?
✓ Which supervisors or mentors can I learn from?
✓ What industry events, conferences, or webinars can I attend?

Step 2: Strengthening Peer Learning

✓ How often do I seek advice from other supervisors?

Rarely
Sometimes
Often

✓ Who are three peers I can reach out to for advice or mentorship?

Step 3: Taking Action

✓ One professional development event I will attend this quarter:
✓ One new connection I will make this month:

Worksheet 5: Encouraging a Learning Culture in Your Team

Purpose: Promote continuous learning among your employees.

Step 1: Evaluate Your Team's Learning Culture

✓ Do my employees feel encouraged to develop new skills?
   ☐ Yes ☐ No
✓ Do I provide opportunities for learning and development?
   ☐ Yes ☐ No
✓ How often do I discuss professional growth with my team?

Rarely
Sometimes
Often

Step 2: Creating a Learning Environment

✓ How can I integrate learning into my team's daily work?
✓ What resources can I provide to help employees develop new skills?
✓ How can I recognize and reward employees who seek continuous improvement?

Step 3: Learning-Focused Leadership

✓ How can I lead by example and demonstrate my own commitment to learning?
✓ What's one way I will show my team that learning is a priority this month?

Checklist: Becoming a Continuous Learner

Purpose: Ensure you stay on track with lifelong learning.

Developing a Growth Mindset

✓ I see challenges as learning opportunities.

✓ I seek feedback and use it to improve.

✓ I embrace change rather than resist it.

Building New Skills

✓ I set learning goals every quarter.

✓ I invest time in professional development (books, courses, training).

✓ I apply new skills and reflect on what I've learned.

Leveraging Learning Resources

✓ I regularly **engage with other supervisors to share best practices.**

✓ **I attend industry events, webinars, or networking groups.**

✓ **I seek ment**orship and professional guidance.

Encouraging a Learning Culture

✓ I model continuous learning for my team.

✓ I create opportunities for employees to share knowledge.

✓ I recognize employees who demonstrate personal growth.

Staying Curious and Adaptable

✓ I actively seek out new perspectives and ideas.

✓ I encourage innovative thinking in my team.

✓ I remain open to change and new ways of doing things.

Reflection: Your Leadership Learning Plan

Purpose: Commit to ongoing personal and professional growth.

Step 1: Identify a Key Learning Takeaway

✓ What is the most important thing I've learned about continuous learning?

Step 2: Set a Long-Term Learning Goal

✓ In the next year, I want to improve my skills in:
✓ The steps I will take to achieve this goal:

Step 3: Commit to Action

✓ One thing I will do in the next 30 days to strengthen my learning mindset:

Final Thought: A Supervisor's Learning Mindset

Supervision is not about having all the answers—**it's about always seeking better questions. Your challenge:** Pick one action from this chapter and apply it immediately. By committing to continuous learning, you will not only **stay relevant as a leader** but **inspire those around you to grow as well.**

Final Leadership Roadmap: Your Supervisor's Growth Plan

Purpose: This checklist and self-assessment will help you review what you've learned, identify areas for continued development, and commit to an action plan for the future.

Part 1: Leadership Self-Assessment

Reflect on your supervisory journey and **rate yourself** on a scale of **1 (Needs Work) to 5 (Confident & Consistent)** in the following areas:

Mindset and Transition

I have fully transitioned from an individual contributor to a leadership mindset. (1–5)

I trust my team to take ownership of tasks rather than micromanaging. (1–5)

I actively seek opportunities to grow as a leader. (1–5)

Building Trust and Team Culture

I foster a culture of openness, trust, and psychological safety. (1–5)

My team feels comfortable bringing challenges and ideas to me. (1–5)

I lead with empathy and create a safe space for learning and failure. (1–5)

Communication and Feedback

I provide clear expectations for my team. (1–5)

I give constructive feedback that promotes learning and improvement. (1–5)

I listen actively and encourage honest, two-way conversations. (1–5)

Time Management and Delegation

I effectively prioritize my workload and delegate tasks appropriately. (1–5)

I balance supporting my team while maintaining my own responsibilities. (1–5)

I focus on strategic leadership rather than getting stuck in day-to-day execution. (1–5)

Performance and Accountability

I regularly set and review performance goals with my team. (1–5)
I handle underperformance constructively, focusing on solutions.
   (1–5)
I encourage self-accountability and ownership within my team.
   (1–5)

Navigating Change and Growth

I help my team navigate change with confidence and resilience.
   (1–5)
I encourage a learning culture and professional development within
   my team. (1–5)
I lead by example, continuously improving my leadership skills.
   (1–5)

Hiring and Team Building

I hire with intention, ensuring new hires align with the team's needs.
   (1–5)
I support new employees with structured onboarding and mentorship. (1–5)
I foster collaboration and cohesion among my team members. (1–5)

Part 2: Identifying Growth Areas

Review your self-assessment.
✓ What **three areas** do I feel most confident in?
✓ What **two areas** do I need to develop further?
✓ What specific steps can I take to improve these areas?

Part 3: 90-Day Leadership Action Plan

Commit to **one action per category** to grow as a leader over the next three months.

Mindset and Transition: One way I will reinforce my leadership mindset:

✓ _____

Building Trust and Culture: One way I will strengthen trust within my team:

✓ _____

Communication and Feedback: One improvement I will make in how I communicate:

✓ _____

Time Management and Delegation: One way I will delegate more effectively:

✓ _____

Performance and Accountability: One strategy I will implement for performance management:

✓ _____

Navigating Change and Growth: One way I will prepare myself and my team for change:

✓ _____

Hiring and Team Building: One thing I will do to improve my team's hiring and development process:

✓ _____

Part 4: Long-Term Leadership Growth Plan

Looking ahead, commit to the following:
✓ A **book, podcast, or course** I will complete in the next 6 months:
✓ A mentorship or peer learning opportunity I will pursue:
✓ A **personal leadership challenge** I will take on in the next year:

Part 5: Leadership Mantra

Write a **leadership statement** that captures your commitment to growth. Example:

> *"I am a leader who builds trust, encourages learning, and leads with clarity and purpose. I will continue to grow, support my team, and strive for excellence—not perfection."*

My leadership mantra:

✓ _____

Final Thought

Your **supervisory journey begins today**—but it **never truly ends.** By setting a plan for continuous improvement, you're ensuring that your leadership will **grow, adapt, and inspire** for years to come. Keep learning, keep leading, and most importantly—**keep showing up for your team.**

   Your journey starts now. Go lead.

References

Introduction

Center for Creative Leadership. 2023. *12 Common Challenges of New Managers.* Center for Creative Leadership.

Drucker, Peter F. 1954. *The Practice of Management.* Harper & Brothers.

Follett, Mary Parker. 1949. *Freedom and Coordination: Lectures in Business Organization.* Management Publications Trust.

Gallup. 2022. *State of the Global Workplace Report.* Gallup Press.

Mayo, Elton. 1949. *The Social Problems of an Industrial Civilization.* Routledge.

Society for Human Resource Management. 2022. *Future of Work: The Skills Gap 2022.* SHRM Research Institute.

Taylor, Frederick Winslow. 1911. *The Principles of Scientific Management.* Harper & Brothers.

Chapter 1: Transitioning to a Supervisory Role

Arruda, William. 2023. "Why Most New Managers Fail and How to Prevent It." *Forbes,* February 15, 2023. https://www.forbes.com/sites/williamarruda/2023/02/15/why-most-new-managers-fail-and-how-to-prevent-it/.

Goleman, Daniel. 1995. *Emotional Intelligence: Why It Can Matter More Than IQ.* Bantam Books.

Ibarra, Herminia, Scott Snook, and Laura Guillen Ramo. 2018. "Identity-Based Leader Development," in *The Nature of Leadership*, ed. D. V. Day and J. Antonakis. 3rd ed. SAGE Publications.

McKinsey & Company. 2021. "The Challenges of Balancing Operational Demands and Strategic Goals," *McKinsey Quarterly.*

PsicoSmart. 2024. "The Impact of Emotional Intelligence on Conflict Resolution Strategies." *PsicoSmart Blog.* https://psico-smart.com/en/blogs/blog-the-impact-of-emotional-intelligence-on-conflict-resolution-strategies-171579.

Quantum Workplace. 2022. "Making Time and Space for Performance Management." July 13, 2022. https://www.quantumworkplace.com/future-of-work/how-much-time-should-a-manager-spend-developing-employees.

TalentSmart. 2023. *The Business Case for Emotional Intelligence (EQ).* Accessed May 16, 2025. https://www.talentsmarteq.com/media/uploads/pdfs/Business_Case_For_Emotional_Intelligence.pdf.

Vorecol. 2024. "The Hidden Link Between Emotional Intelligence and Employee Productivity: What Companies Are Overlooking." *Vorecol Blog*. https://vorecol.com/blogs/blog-the-hidden-link-between-emotional-intelligence-and-employee-productivity-what-companies-are-overlooking-201286.

Chapter 2: Building Trust and Rapport with Your Team

Harvard Business Publishing. 2022. "How Leaders Build Trust." *Harvard Business Review*. Accessed May 16, 2025. https://s.hbr.org/45JCrjM.

Kemp, Andy. 2024. "Most Unethical Behavior Goes Unreported and Unresolved." *Gallup*. May 2024. https://www.gallup.com/workplace/648770/unethical-behavior-goes-unreported-unresolved.aspx.

McKinsey & Company. 2023. *The State of Organizations 2023: Ten Shifts Transforming Organizations*. April 26, 2023. https://www.mckinsey.com/capabilities/people-and-organizational-performance/our-insights/the-state-of-organizations-2023.

Vodicka, Devin. 2020. "The Four Elements of Trust." *Learner-Centered Leadership*, August 8, 2020. https://learnercenteredleadership.org/2020/08/08/the-four-elements-of-trust/.

Chapter 3: Setting Clear Expectations and Providing Feedback

Gallup. 2021. *How Effective Feedback Fuels Performance*. Gallup Workplace. https://www.gallup.com/workplace/357764/fast-feedback-fuels-performance.aspx.

Gallup. 2023. *The Role of Clear Expectations in Driving Employee Engagement and Productivity*. Gallup Press.

Lencioni, Patrick. 2002. *The Five Dysfunctions of a Team: A Leadership Fable*. Jossey-Bass.

McKinsey & Company. 2024. ."The Science of Productive Feedback: Enhancing Manager-Employee Communication in 2024," *McKinsey Quarterly*.

Chapter 4: Managing Time and Priorities

Gallup. 2017. *The State of the American Workplace: Employee Engagement Insights for U.S. Business Leaders*. Gallup Press.

Gallup. 2023. *Time Management and Employee Productivity: Understanding the Relationship Between Prioritization and Engagement*. Gallup Press.

McKinsey & Company. 2023. *The State of Organizations 2023: Ten Shifts Transforming Organizations*. April 26, 2023. https://www.mckinsey.com /capabilities/people-and-organizational-performance/our-insights/the-state -of-organizations-2023

Ng, Gorick. 2024. *Why the 'Eisenhower Matrix' Is a Fantastic Productivity Hack*. Big Think, July 29, 2024. https://bigthink.com/the-learning-curve/why-the -eisenhower-matrix-is-a-fantastic-productivity-hack/ Accessed September 2024

Proaction International. 2021. "Time Management: The Ideal Distribution of Tasks in a Manager's Day." *Proaction International Blog*. Accessed November 2024. https://blog.proactioninternational.com/en/time-management-ideal -distribution-of-tasks-in-managers-day.

Chapter 5: Delegating Effectively

Bohns, Vanessa K., and Francis J. Flynn. 2021. "Why Didn't You Just Ask? Underestimating the Discomfort of Help-Seeking." *Journal of Experimental Social Psychology* 95: 104137.

Covey, Stephen R. 1989. *The 7 Habits of Highly Effective People*. Free Press.

Rozovsky, Julia, and Abeer Hoffman. 2019. "The Five Keys to a Successful Google Team." *Harvard Business Review Digital Articles* (February): 1-6.

Watkins, Michael D. 2012. "How Managers Become Leaders." *Harvard Business Review*, June 2012.

Chapter 6: Resolving Conflicts and Handling Difficult Conversations

Behfar, Kristin J., Randall S. Peterson, Elizabeth A. Mannix, and William M. K. Trochim. 2022. "The Critical Role of Conflict Resolution in Teams: A Close Look at the Links Between Conflict Type, Conflict Management Strategies, and Team Outcomes." *Journal of Applied Psychology* 107(7): 1088–1111.

CPP Inc. 2008. *Workplace Conflict and How Businesses Can Harness It to Thrive*. CPP Global Human Capital Report.

De Dreu, Carsten K. W., and Laurie R. Weingart. 2021. "A Contingency Theory of Task Conflict and Performance in Groups and Organizational Teams." *Journal of Organizational Behavior* 42(6): 721–742.

Edmondson, Amy C., and J. Richard Dillon. 2023. "The Benefits of Psychological Safety Across Boundaries: Evidence from Global Teams." *Organization Science* 34(1): 170–194.

Edmondson, A. C., and D. M. Smith. 2006. "Too Hot to Handle? How to Manage Relationship Conflict." *California Management Review* 49(1): 6–31.

Maxfield, David, Joseph Grenny, Ron Mcmillan, Kerry Patterson, and Al Switzler. 2013. *Crucial Accountability: Tools for Resolving Violated Expectations, Broken Commitments, and Bad Behavior.* McGraw-Hill Education.

Society for Human Resource Management. 2019. *SHRM/Globoforce Employee Recognition Survey: Designing Work Cultures for the Human Era.* SHRM.

Chapter 7: Supporting Team Development and Growth

Bersin & Associates. 2010. *High-Impact Learning Culture: The 40 Best Practices for Creating an Empowered Enterprise.* Bersin & Associates.

Deloitte (2017). *Global Human Capital Trends 2017: Rewriting the Rules for the Digital Age.* https://www2.deloitte.com/insights/us/en/focus/human-capital -trends/2017.html

Gallup. 2020. *State of the Global Workplace: 2020 Report.* Gallup Press.

LinkedIn. 2019. *2019 Workplace Learning Report: Why 2019 is the Breakout Year for the Talent Developer.* LinkedIn Learning Solutions.

McKinsey & Company. 2021. *The State of Organizations 2021: Transforming With a Human-Centric Approach.* https://www.mckinsey.com/business-functions /organization/our-insights/the-state-of-organizations-2021

Pentland, Alex. 2012. "The New Science of Building Great Teams." *Harvard Business Review*, April 2012. https://hbr.org/2012/04/the-new-science -of-building-great-teams

Chapter 8: Navigating Change and Uncertainty

Fosslien, Liz, and Mollie West Duffy. 2022. *Stop Telling Employees to Be Resilient.* MIT Sloan Management Review. https://sloanreview.mit.edu/article/stop -telling-employees-to-be-resilient/.

Harvard Kennedy School. 2023. *Holding Environments and Public Problem-Solving.* Case Program, Harvard University. https://case.hks.harvard.edu /holding-environments-and-public-problem-solving/.

Heifetz, Ronald A., and Marty Linsky. 2002. *Leadership on the Line: Staying Alive Through the Dangers of Leading.* Boston: Harvard Business Review Press.

Kaplan, Robert S., and David P. Norton. 1992. "The Balanced Scorecard—Measures That Drive Performance." *Harvard Business Review*, January–February 1992. https://hbr.org/1992/01/the-balanced-scorecard-measures -that-drive-performance.

Kotter, John P. 2012. *Leading Change.* Harvard Business Review Press.

Landry, Lauren. 2019. "Emotional Intelligence in Leadership: Why It's Important." *Harvard Business School Online.* https://online.hbs.edu/blog /post/emotional-intelligence-in-leadership.

McKinsey & Company. 2023a. *Going All In: Why Employee 'will' Can Make or Break Transformations.* https://www.mckinsey.com/capabilities /transformation/our-insights/going-all-in-why-employee-will-can-make-or -break-transformations.

McKinsey & Company. 2023b. *The State of Organizations 2023: Ten Shifts Transforming Organizations.* https://www.mckinsey.com/capabilities/people -and-organizational-performance/our-insights/the-state-of-organizations -2023.

McKinsey & Company. 2015. *Changing Change Management.* https://www .mckinsey.com/featured-insights/leadership/changing-change-management.

Prosci. 2022. *Understanding Resistance—Prosci's Flight and Risk Model.* https:// www.prosci.com/blog/understanding-resistance-to-change.

Prosci. 2023. *Change Management Success: What Research Shows.* https://www .prosci.com/change-management-success.

Prosci. 2024a. *The Correlation Between Change Management and Project Success.* https://www.prosci.com/blog/the-correlation-between-change-management -and-project-success.

Prosci. 2024b. *Change Management.* https://www.prosci.com/change-management

Chapter 11: Leading with Empathy and Allowing Space to Fail

Harvard Business Review. 2023. *It's OK to Fail, but You Have to Do It Right.* July 28, 2023. https://hbr.org/2023/07/its-ok-to-fail-but-you-have-to-do-it-right.

McKinsey & Company. 2024. *It's Cool to Be Kind: The Value of Empathy at Work.* February 28, 2024. https://www.mckinsey.com/capabilities/people -and-organizational-performance/our-insights/its-cool-to-be-kind-the-value -of-empathy-at-work.

About the Author

Jeff Ogren brings over 25 years of international leadership and management experience, guiding diverse teams across cultures and continents. His multifaceted career spans military service in the U.S. Army, Peace Corps, procurement management, education, and aviation, while living and working in Japan, Ecuador, United Arab Emirates, Lithuania, Canada, Sweden, and Jordan. While serving as Deputy Director of Management Training at the George P. Shultz National Foreign Affairs Training Center, he developed and delivered transformative training programs in crucial conversations, performance management, and leadership excellence. Jeff holds a BA in political science from Illinois State University and an MPA from the University of Arizona's Eller School of Management.

Index

www.ingramcontent.com/pod-product-compliance
Lightning Source LLC
Chambersburg PA
CBHW061135220326
41599CB00025B/4237